Coloring Book For Adults No Bleed

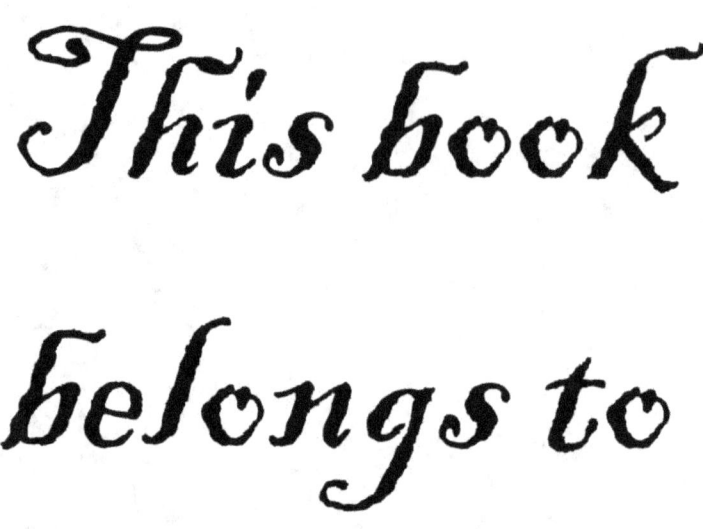

This book

belongs to

....

....

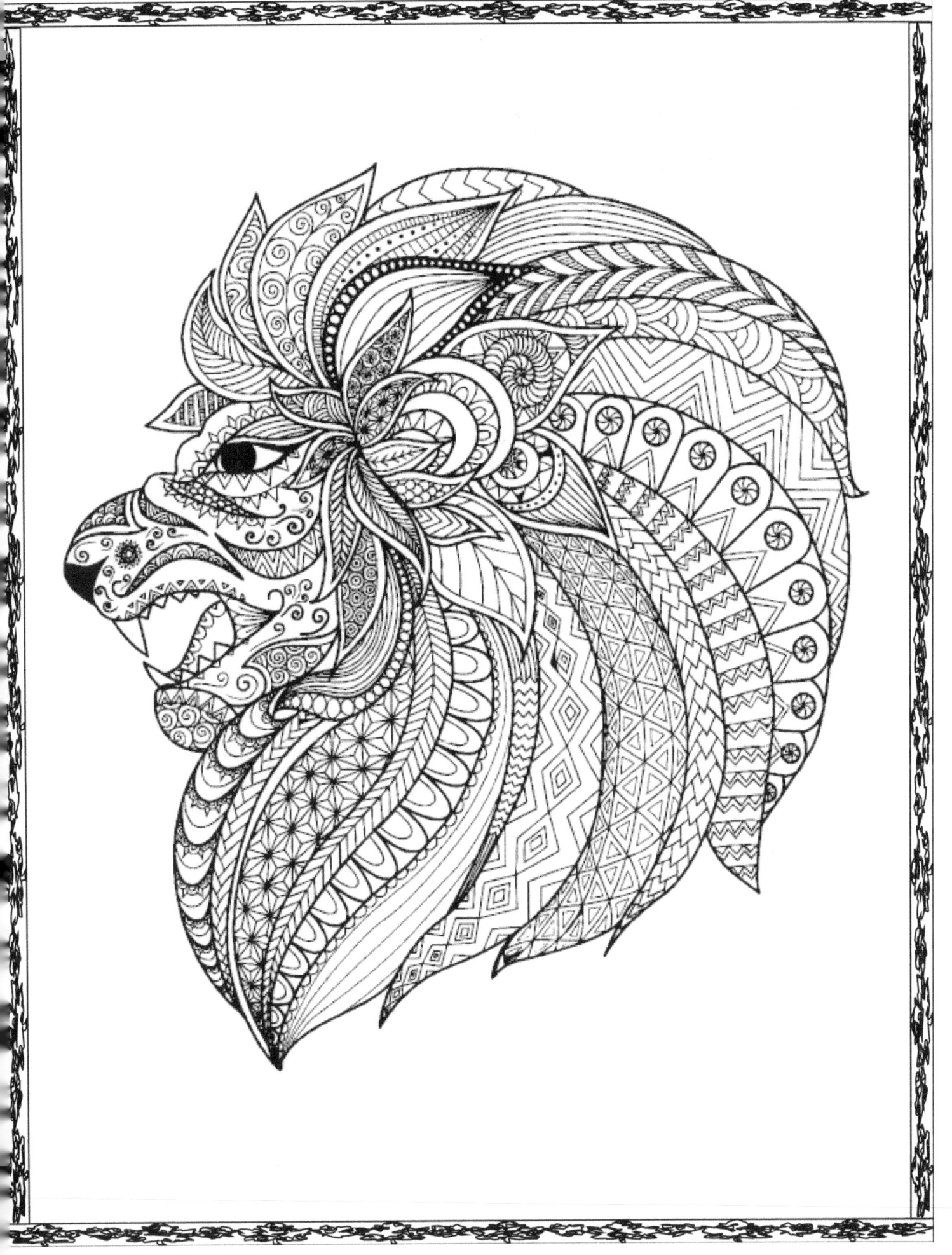

TEST YOUR COLOR

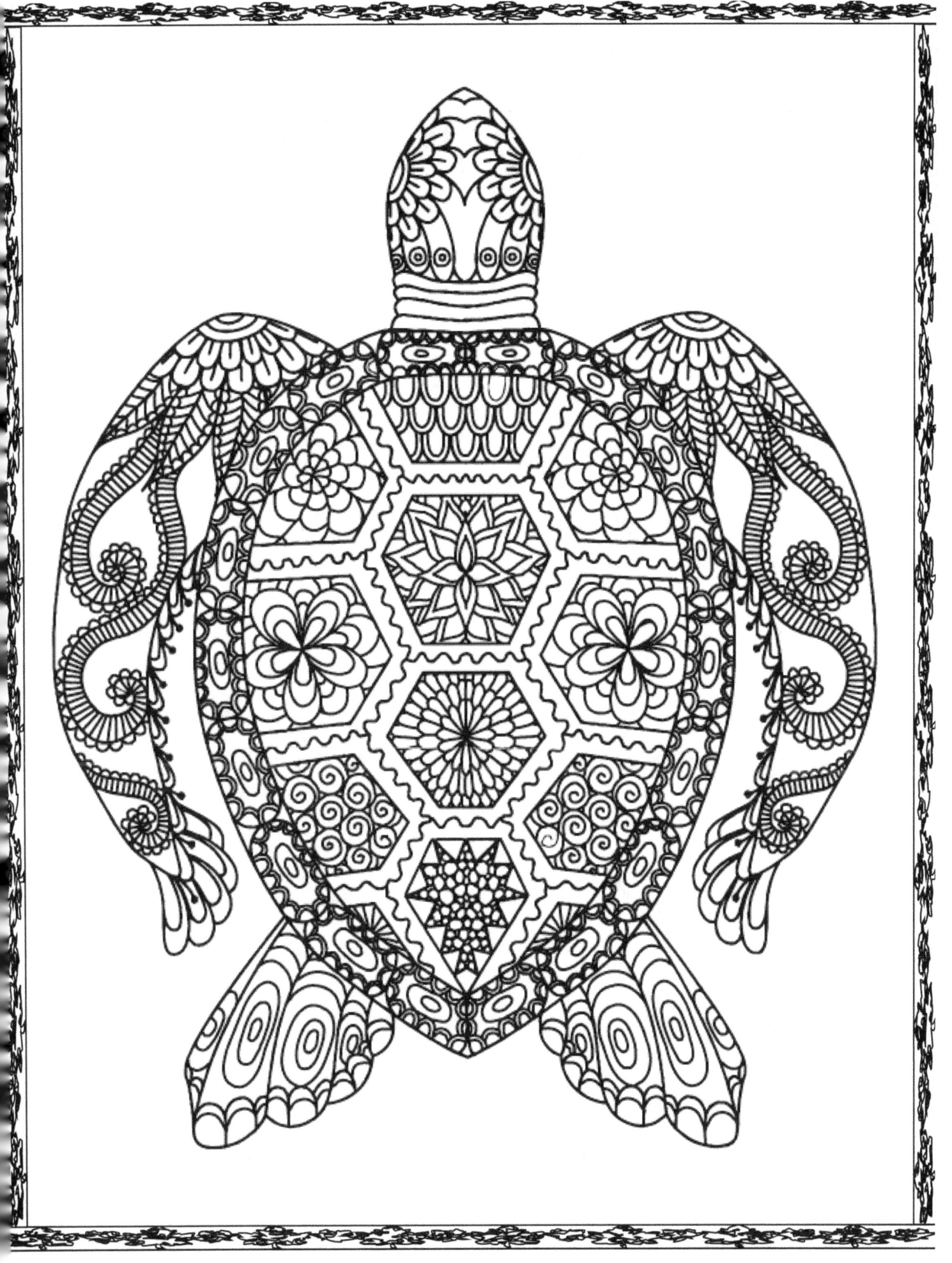

TEST YOUR COLOR

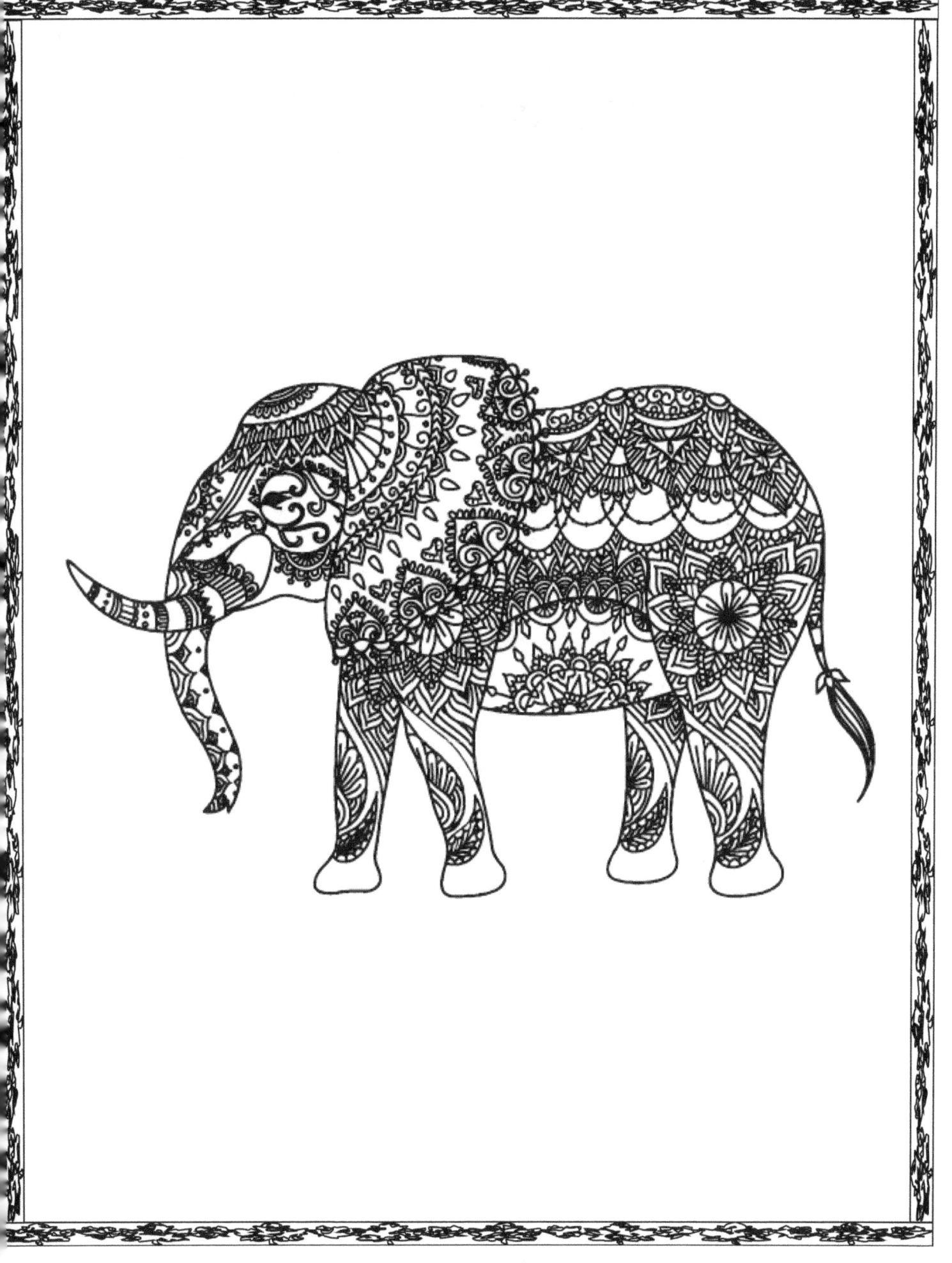

TEST YOUR COLOR

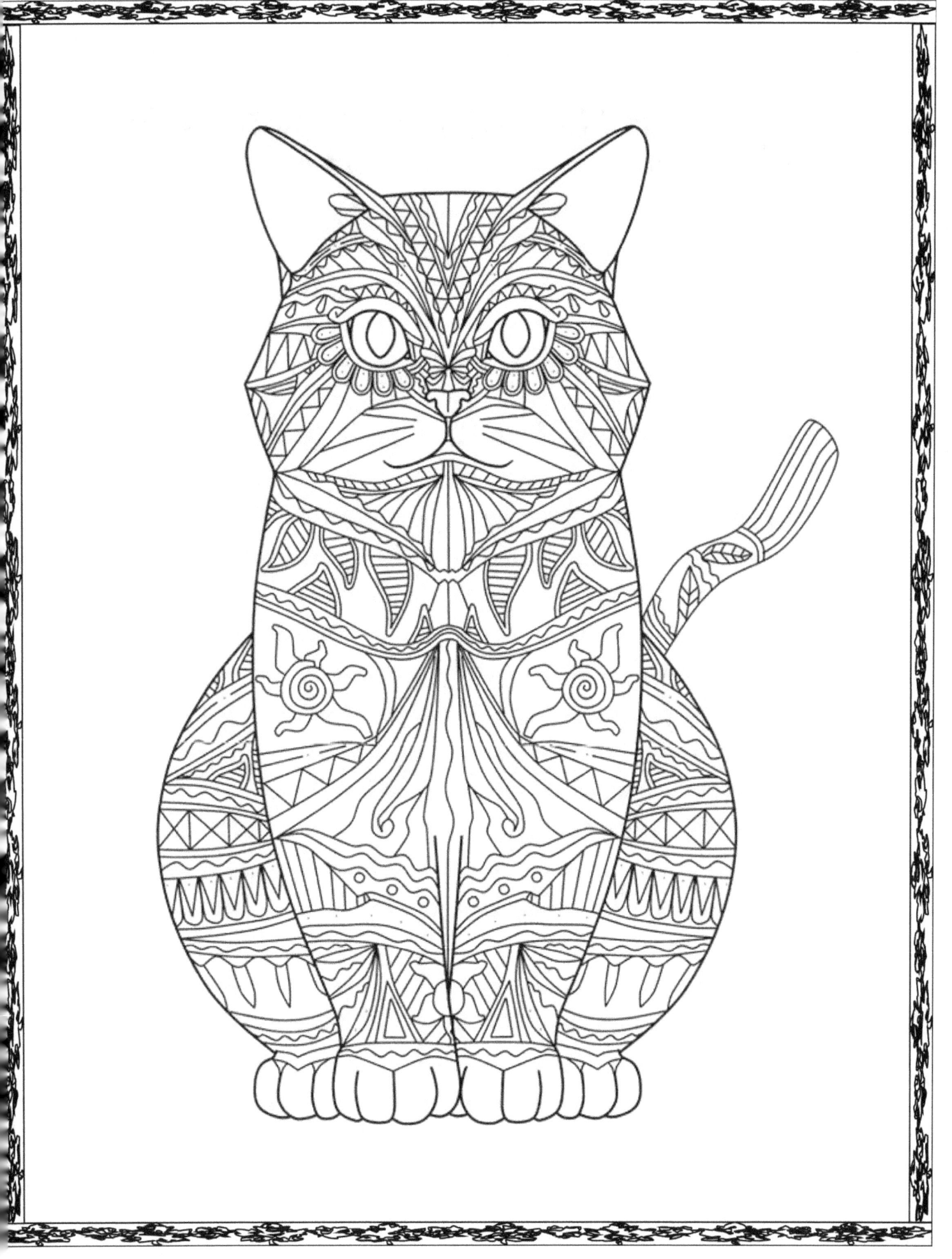

TEST YOUR COLOR

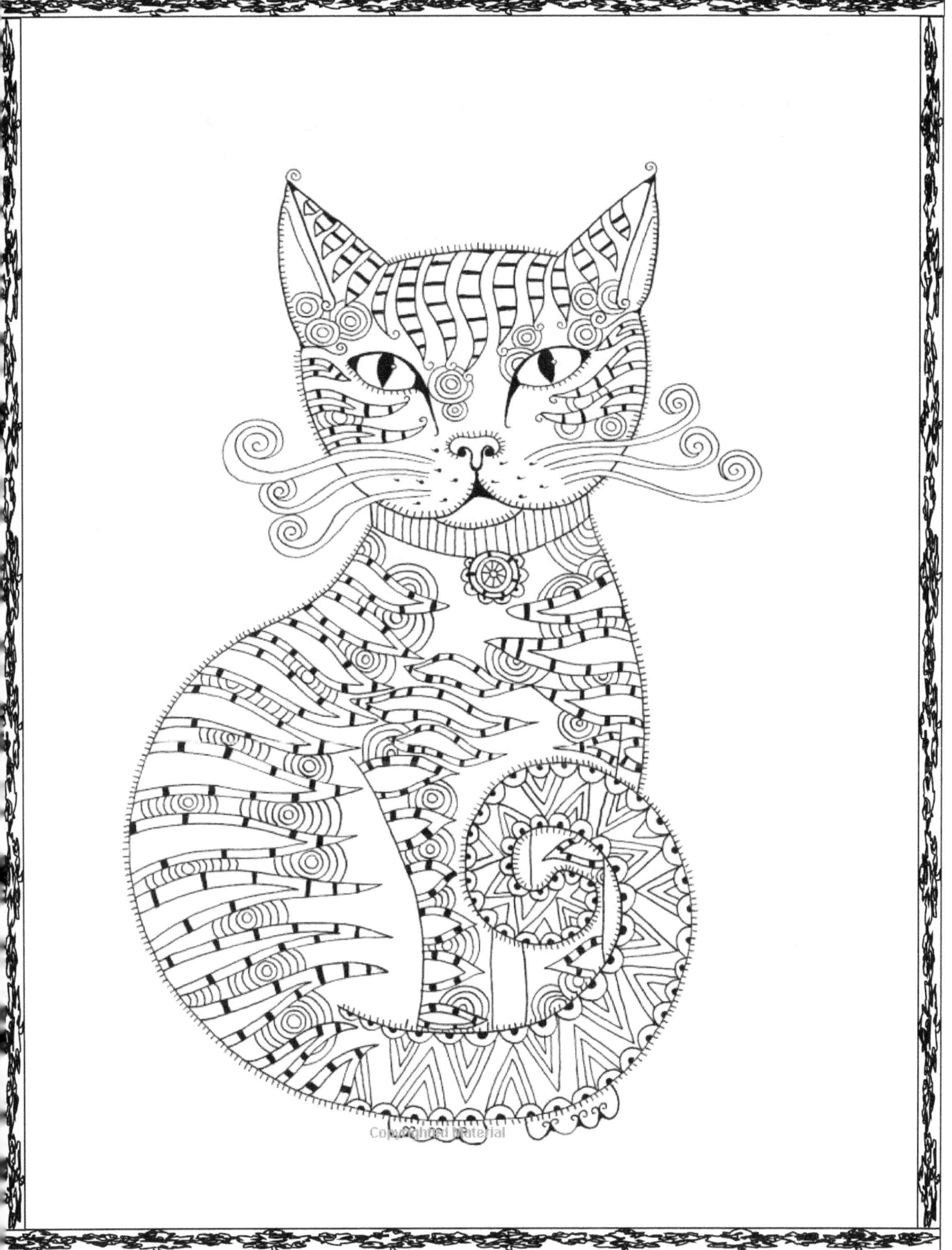

TEST YOUR COLOR

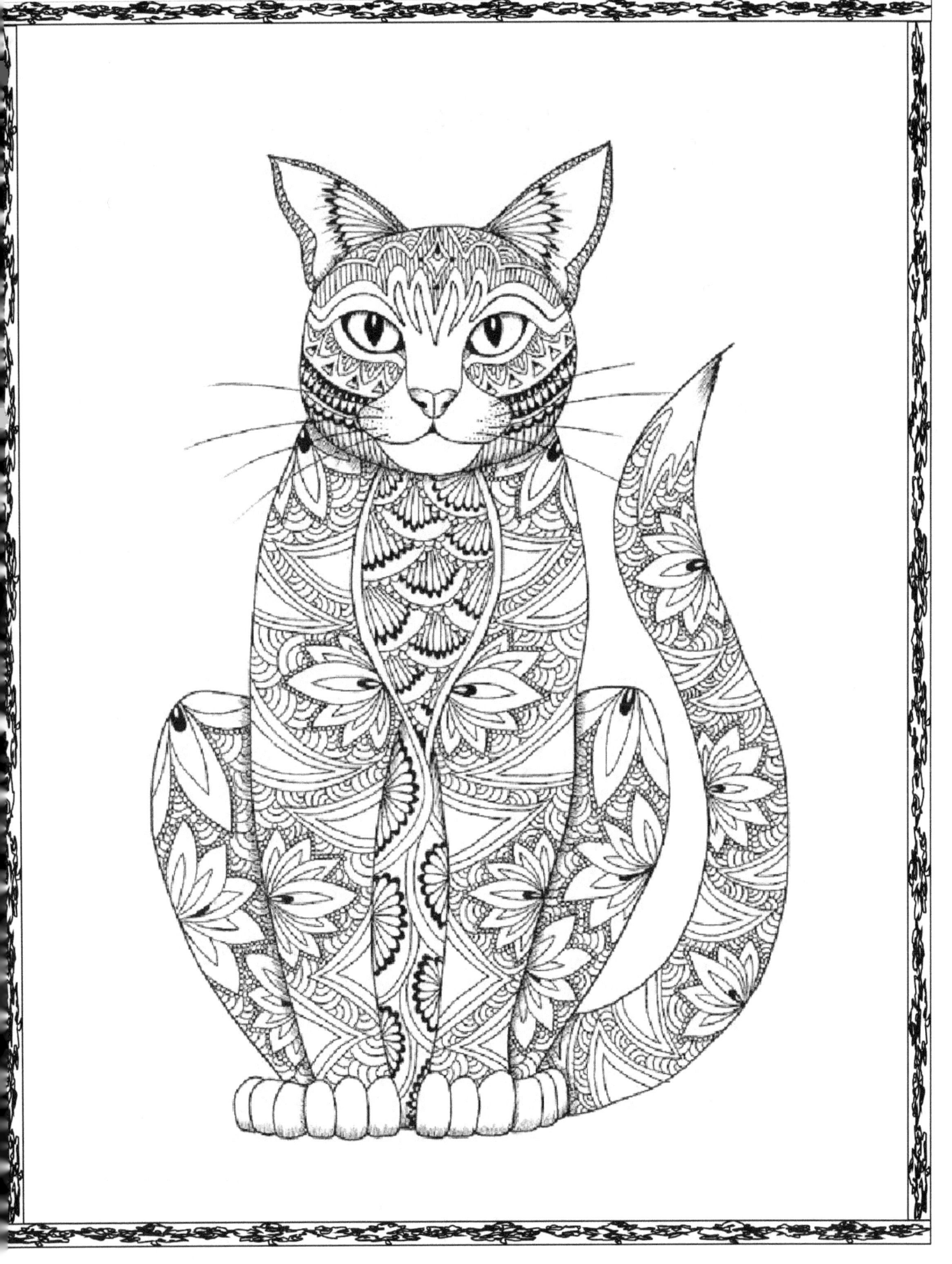

TEST YOUR COLOR

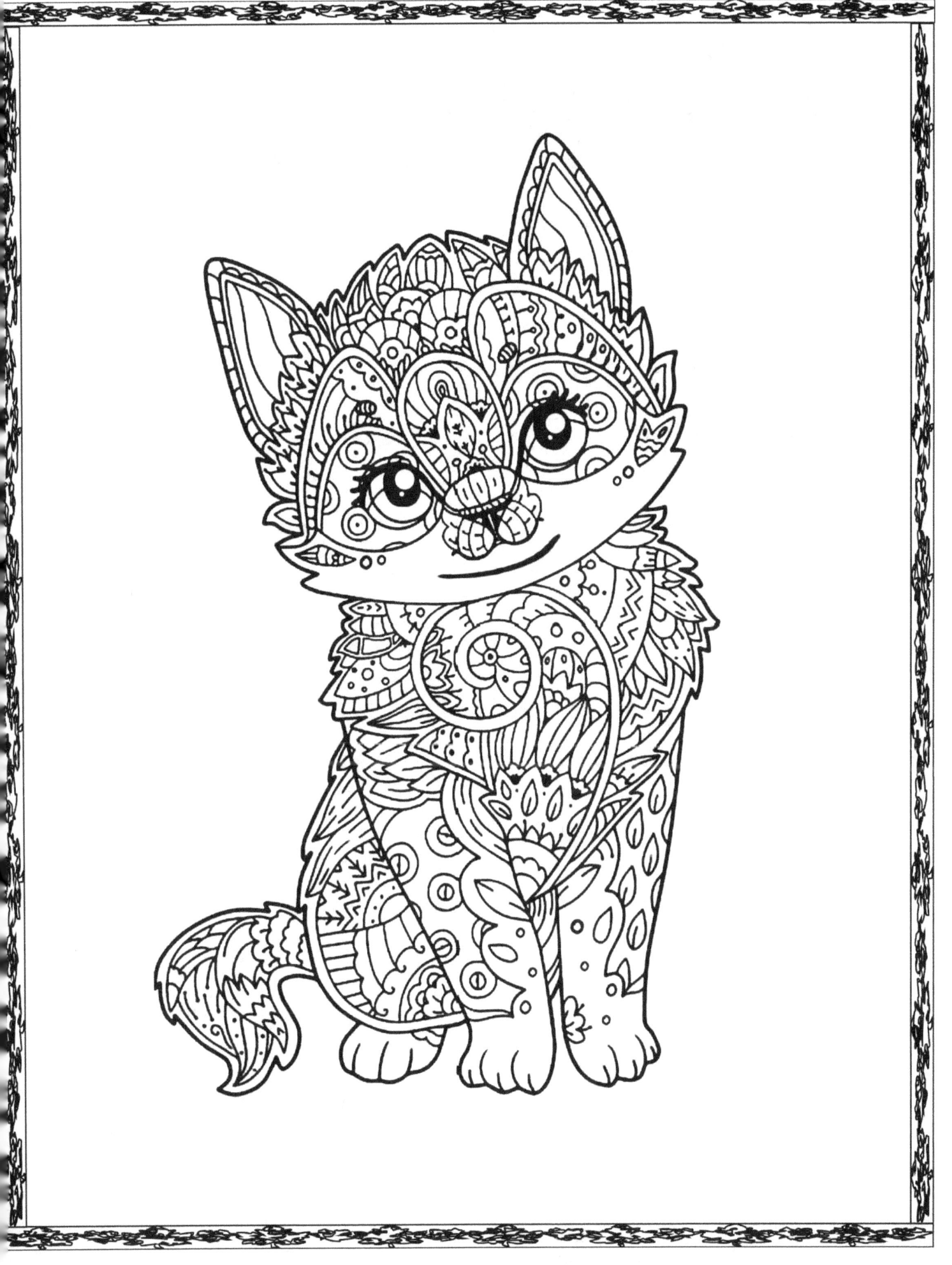

TEST YOUR COLOR

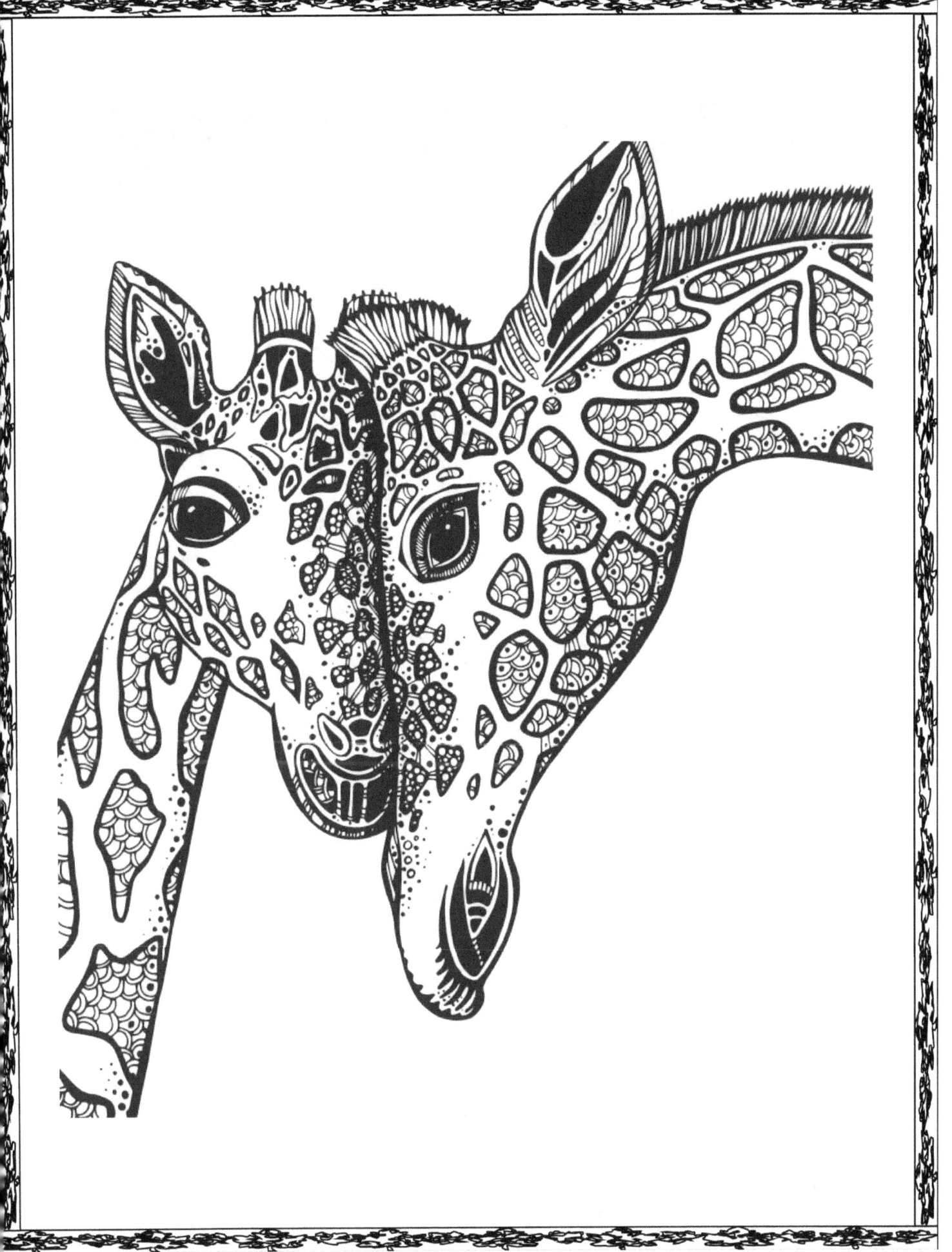

TEST YOUR COLOR

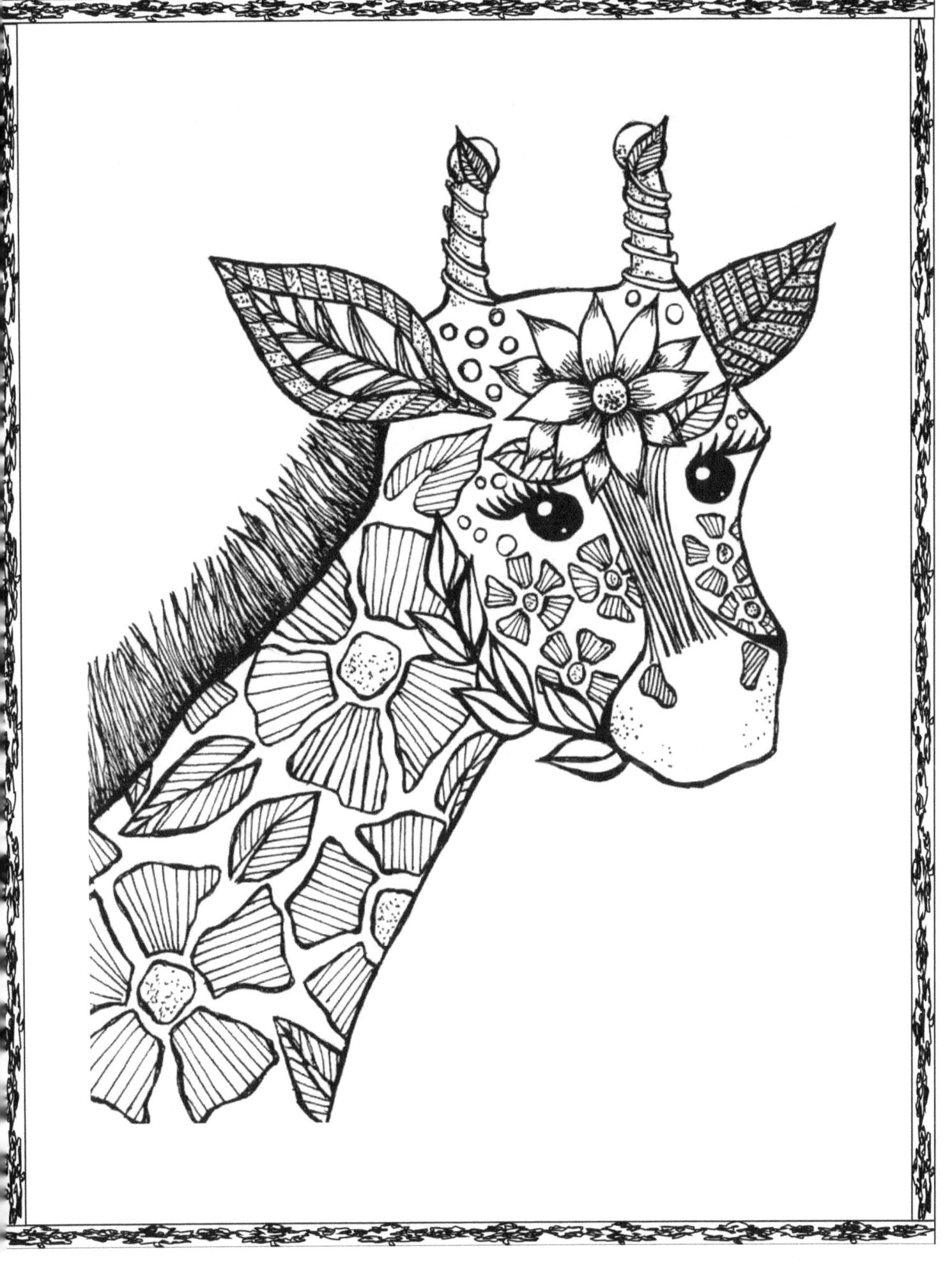

TEST YOUR COLOR

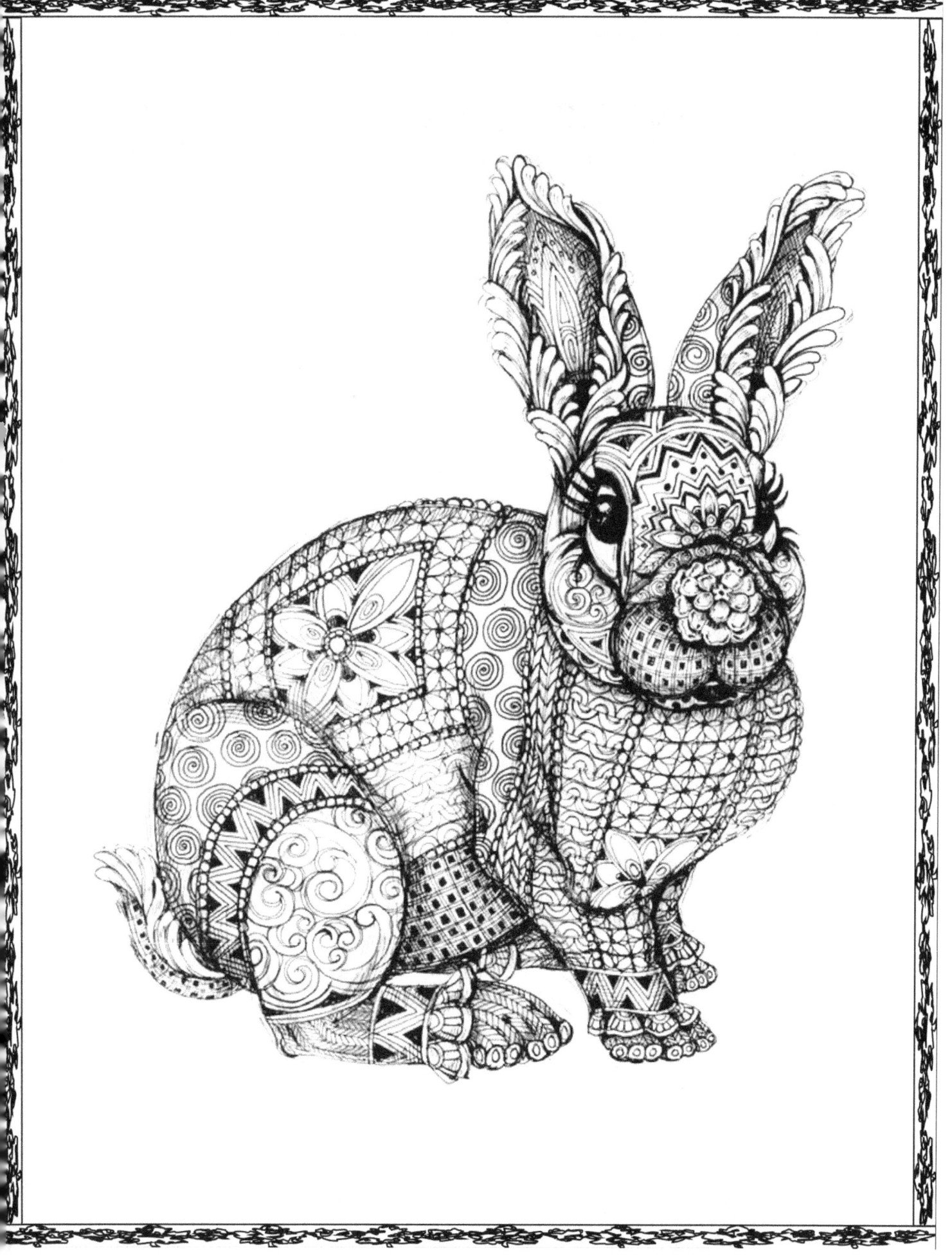

TEST YOUR COLOR

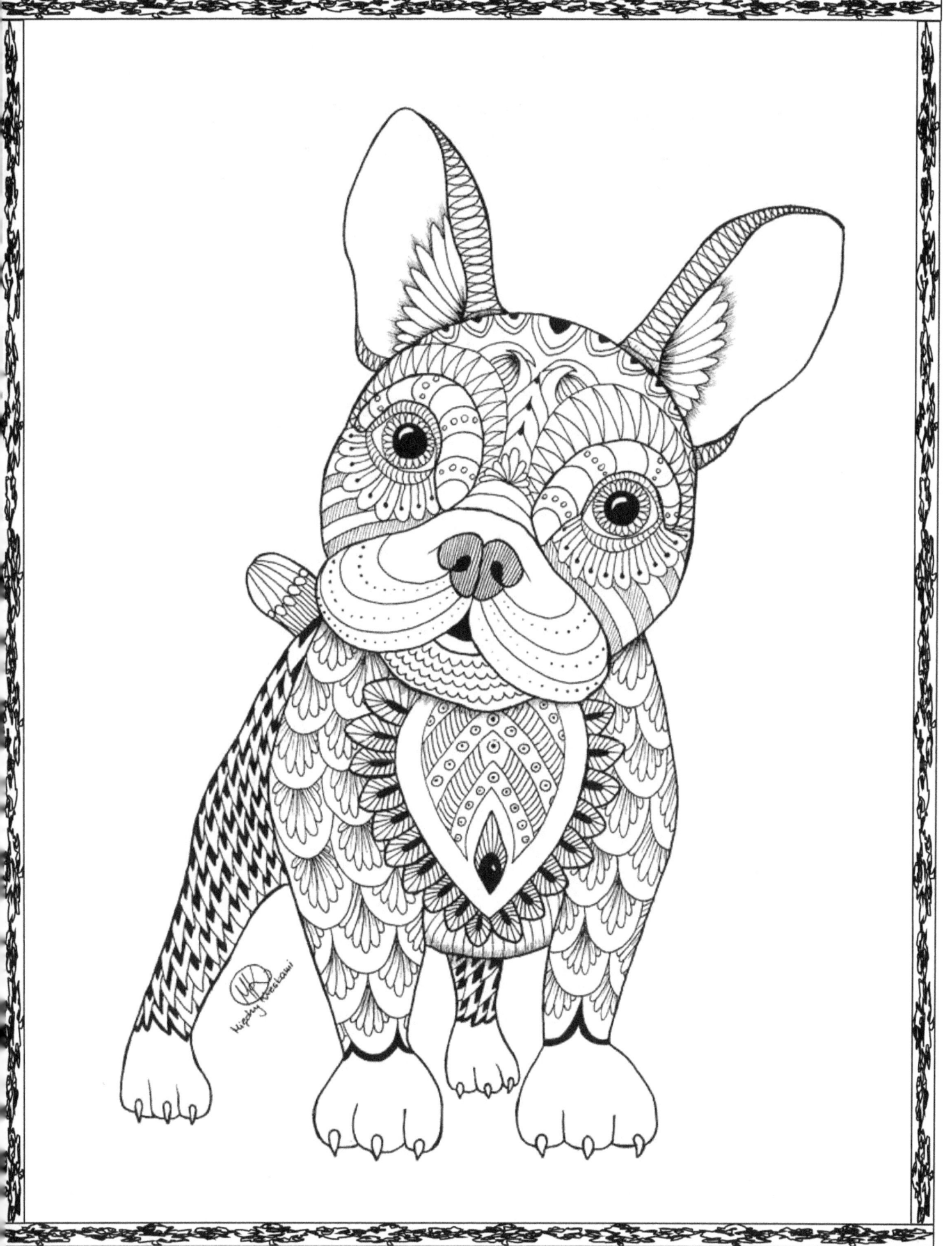

TEST YOUR COLOR

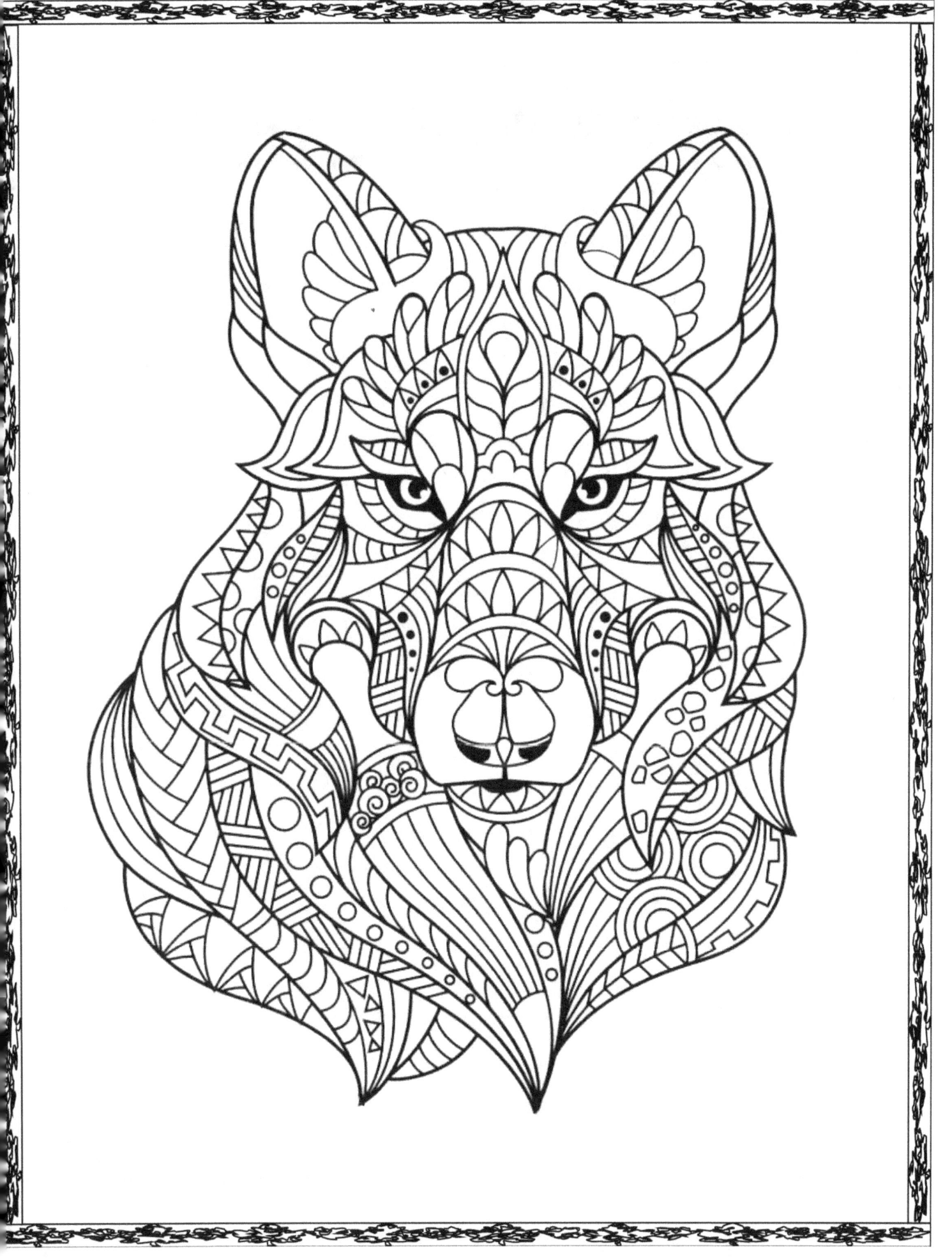

TEST YOUR COLOR

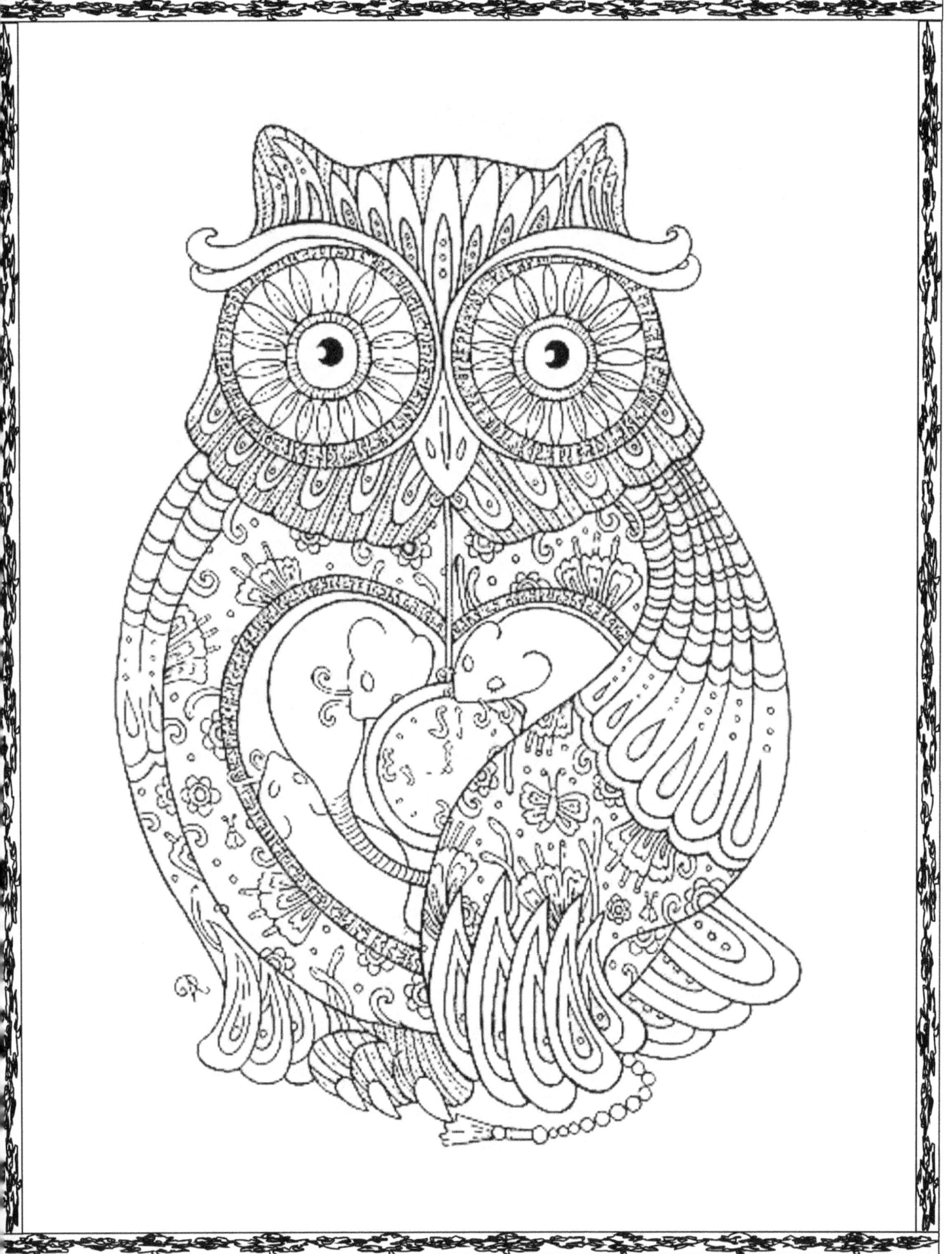

TEST YOUR COLOR

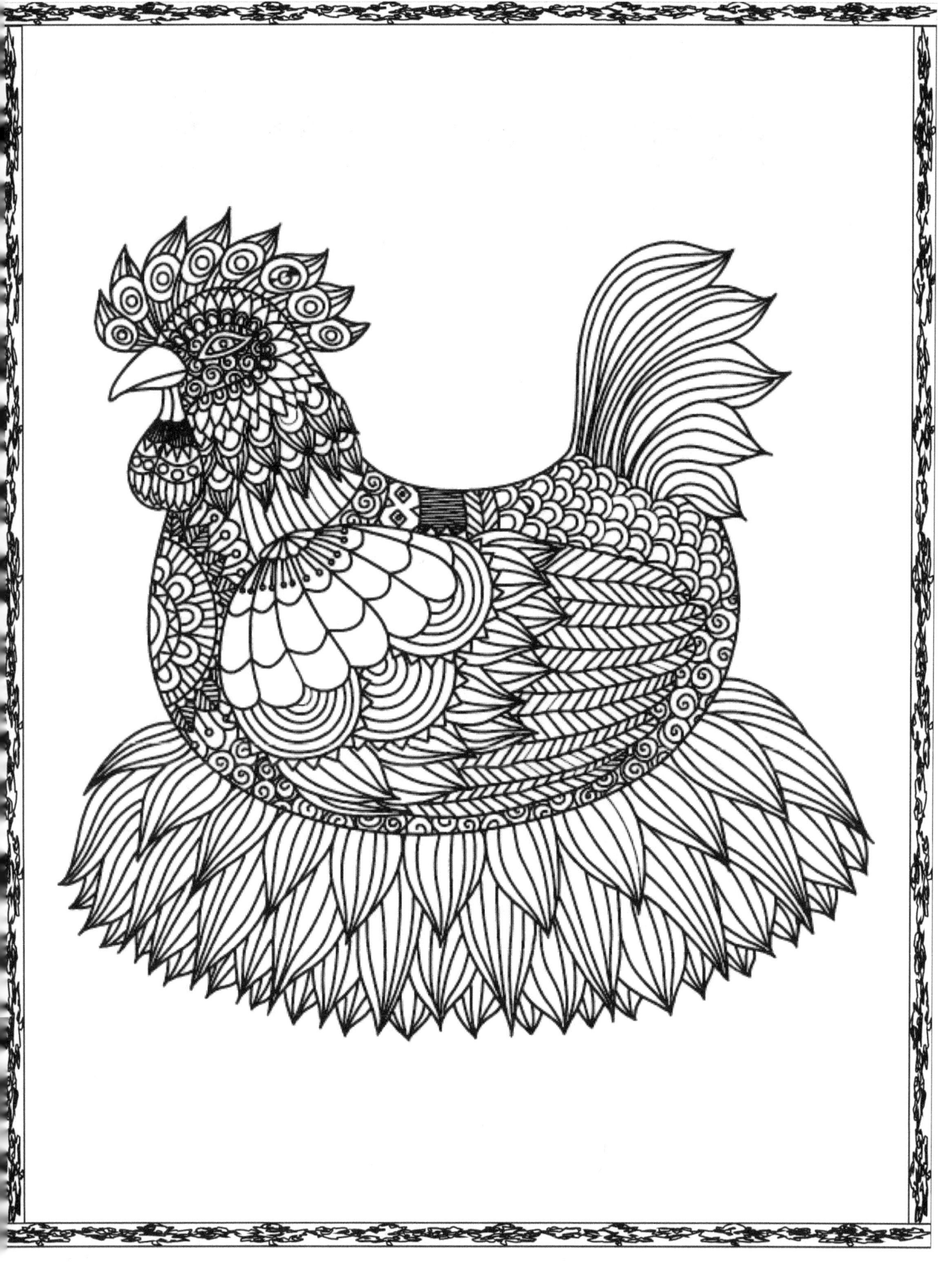

TEST YOUR COLOR

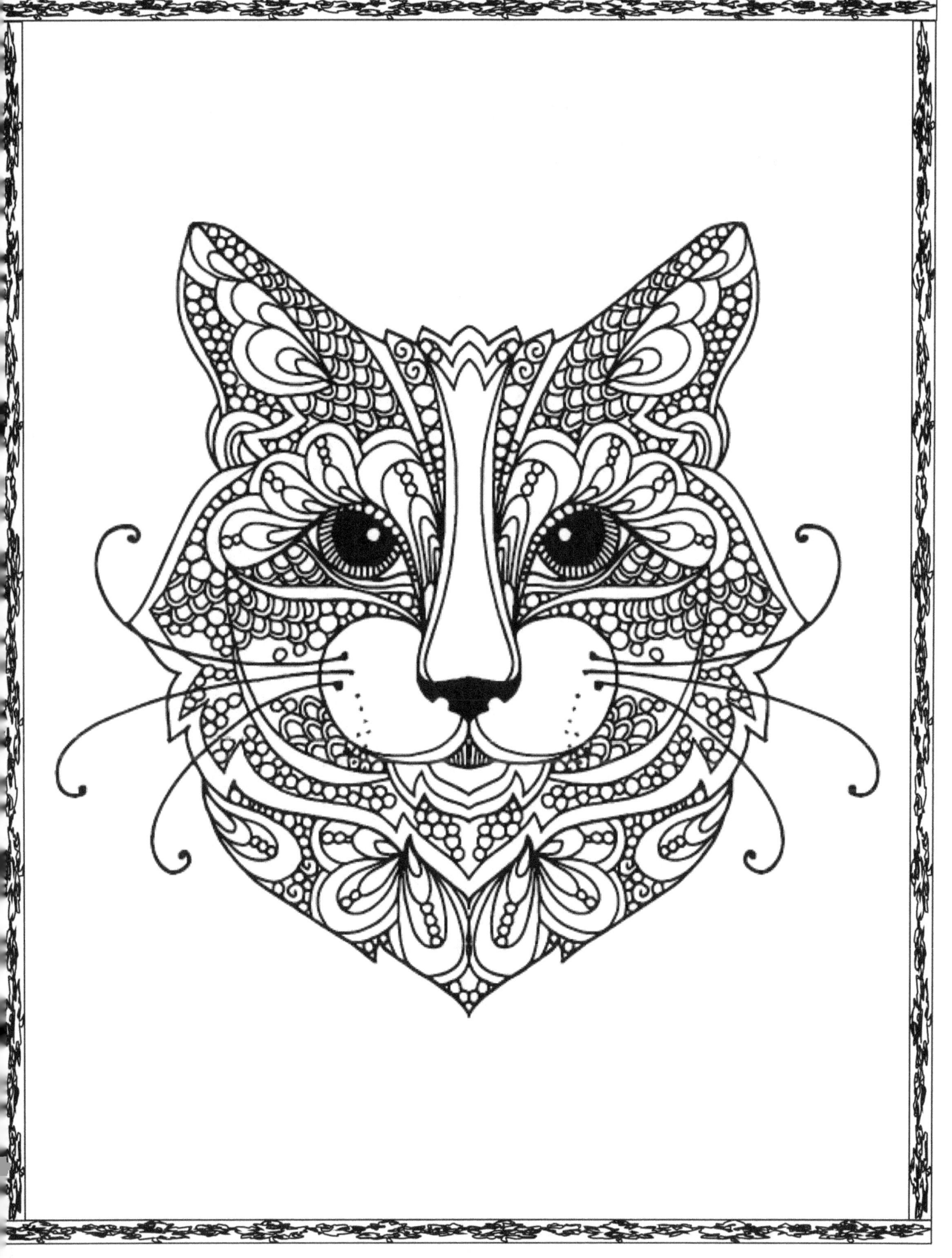

TEST YOUR COLOR

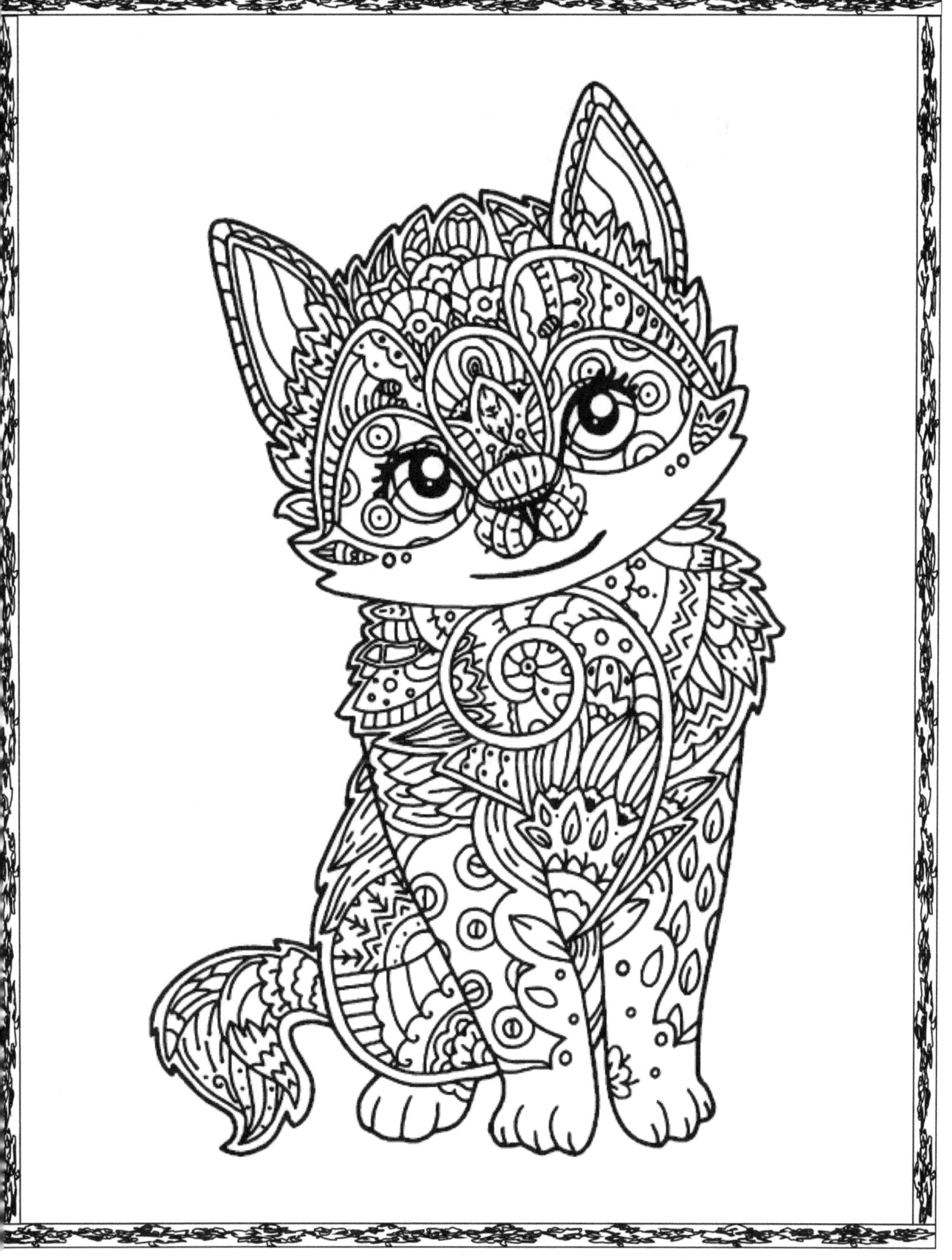

TEST YOUR COLOR

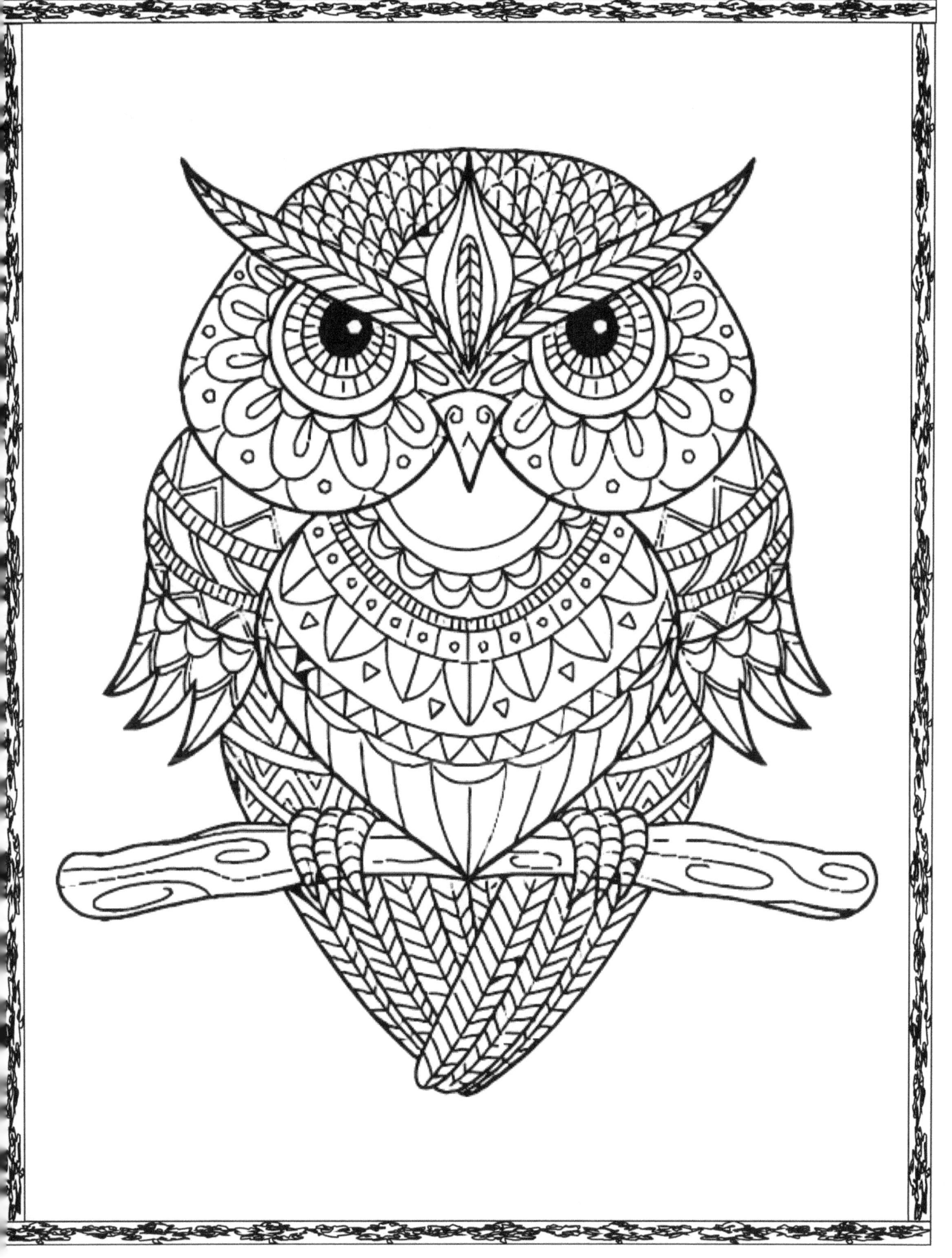

TEST YOUR COLOR

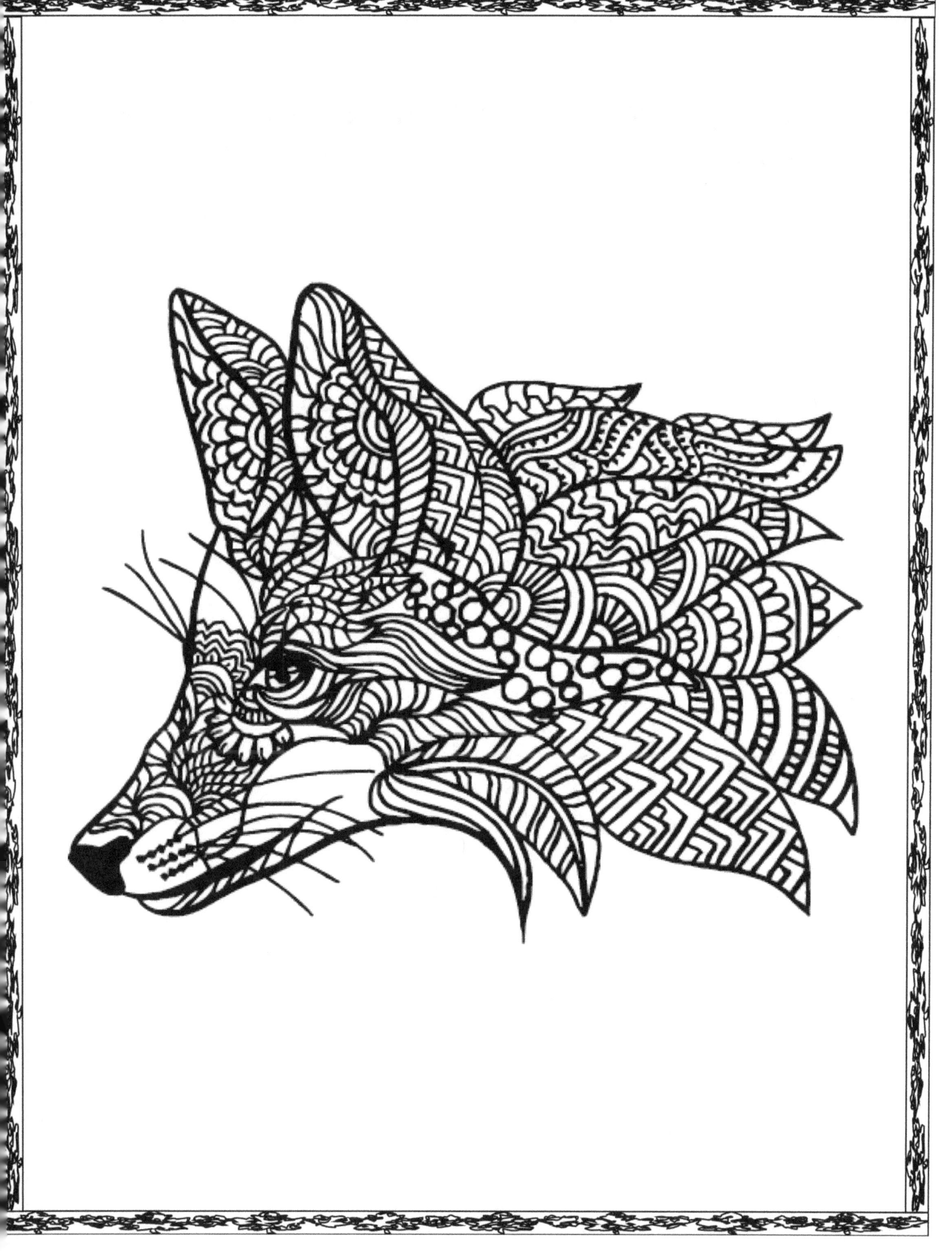

TEST YOUR COLOR

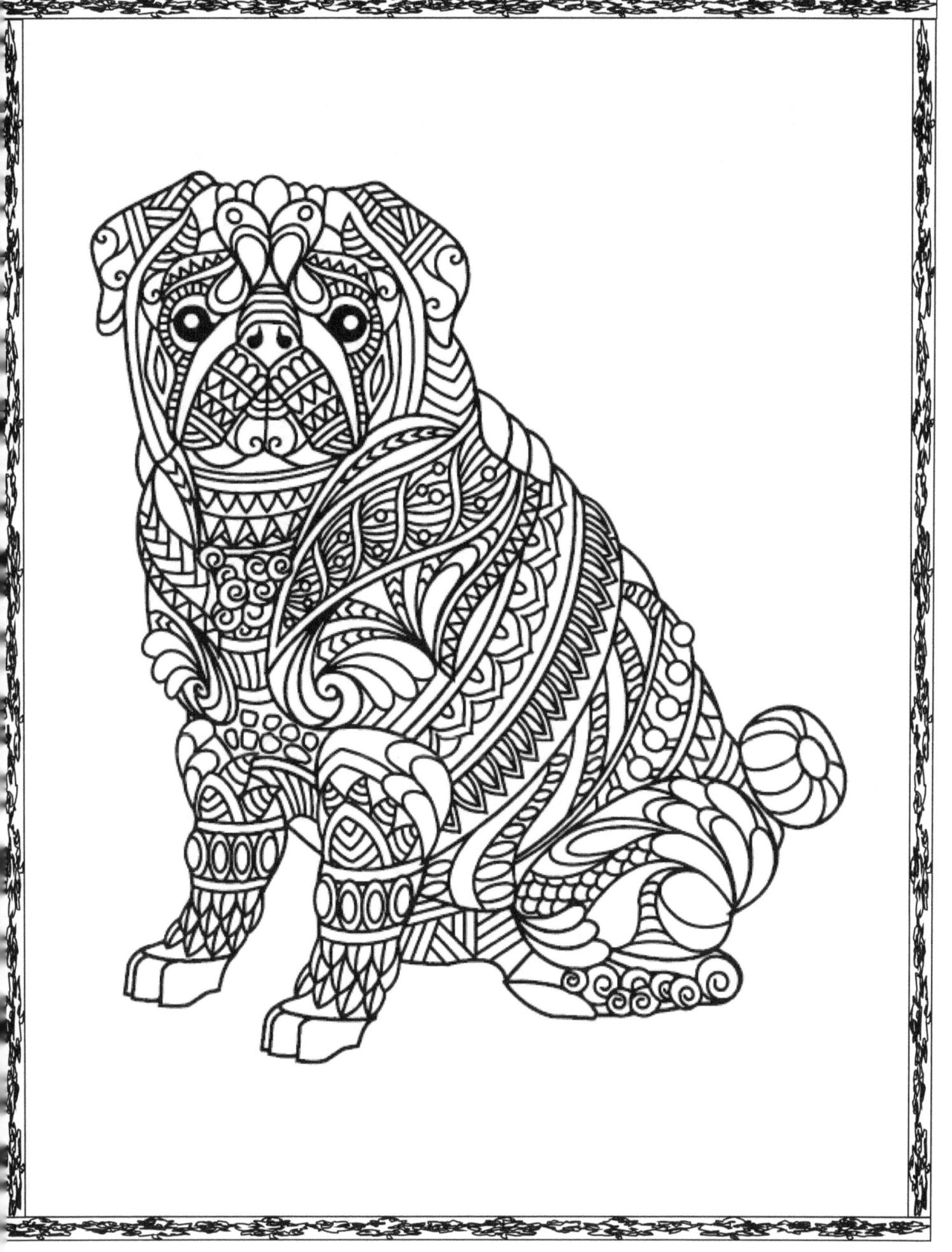

TEST YOUR COLOR

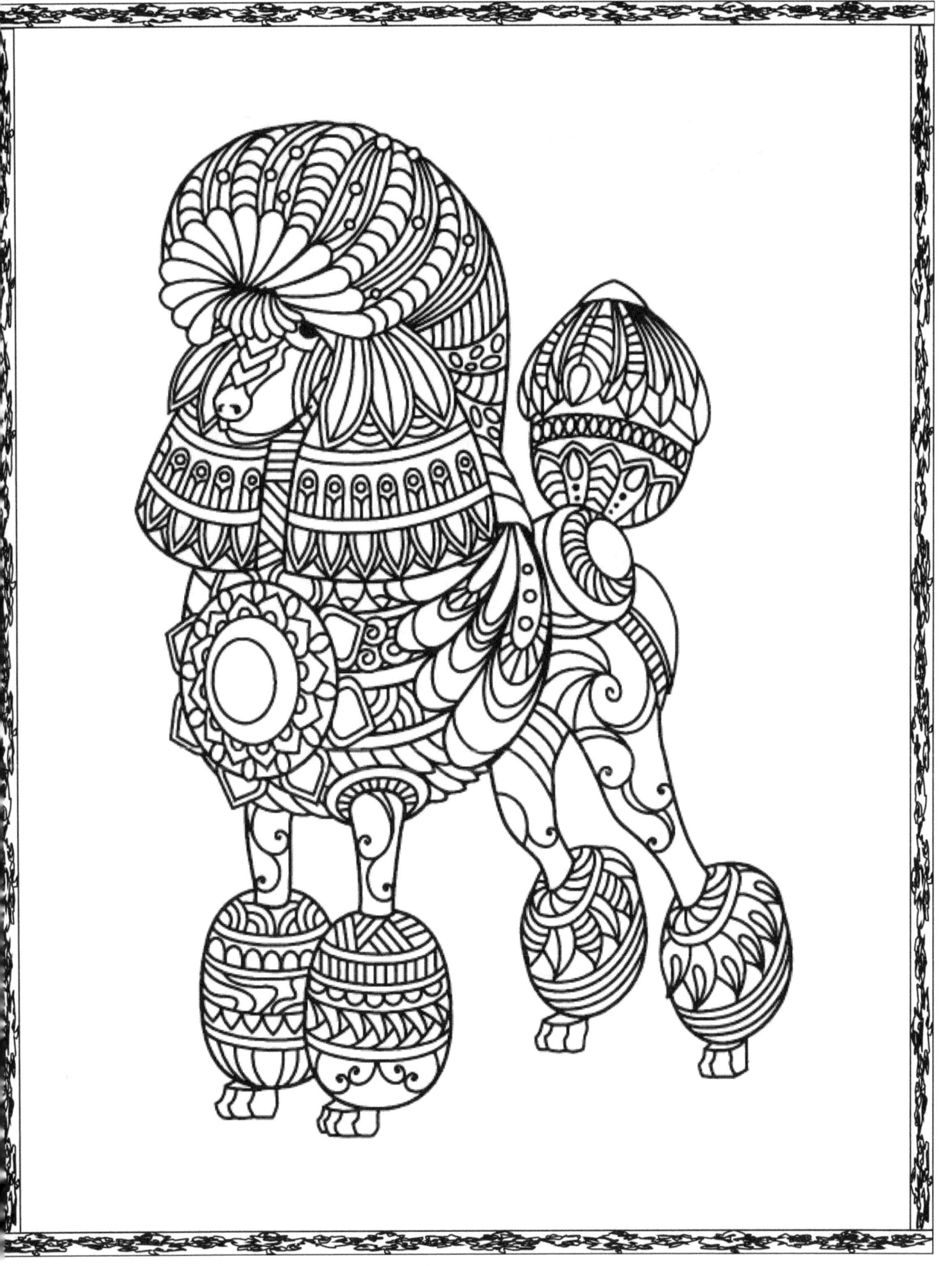

TEST YOUR COLOR

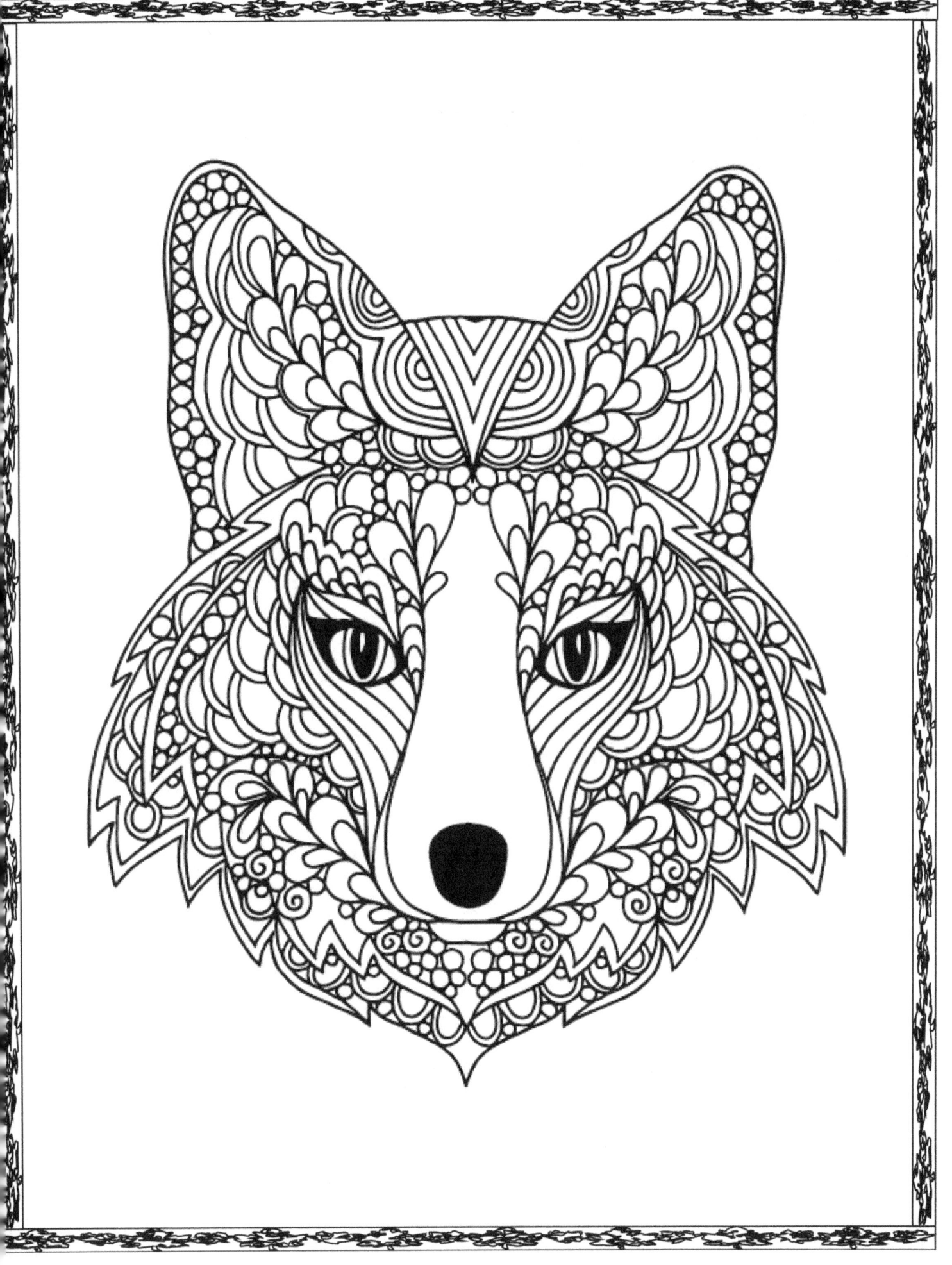

TEST YOUR COLOR

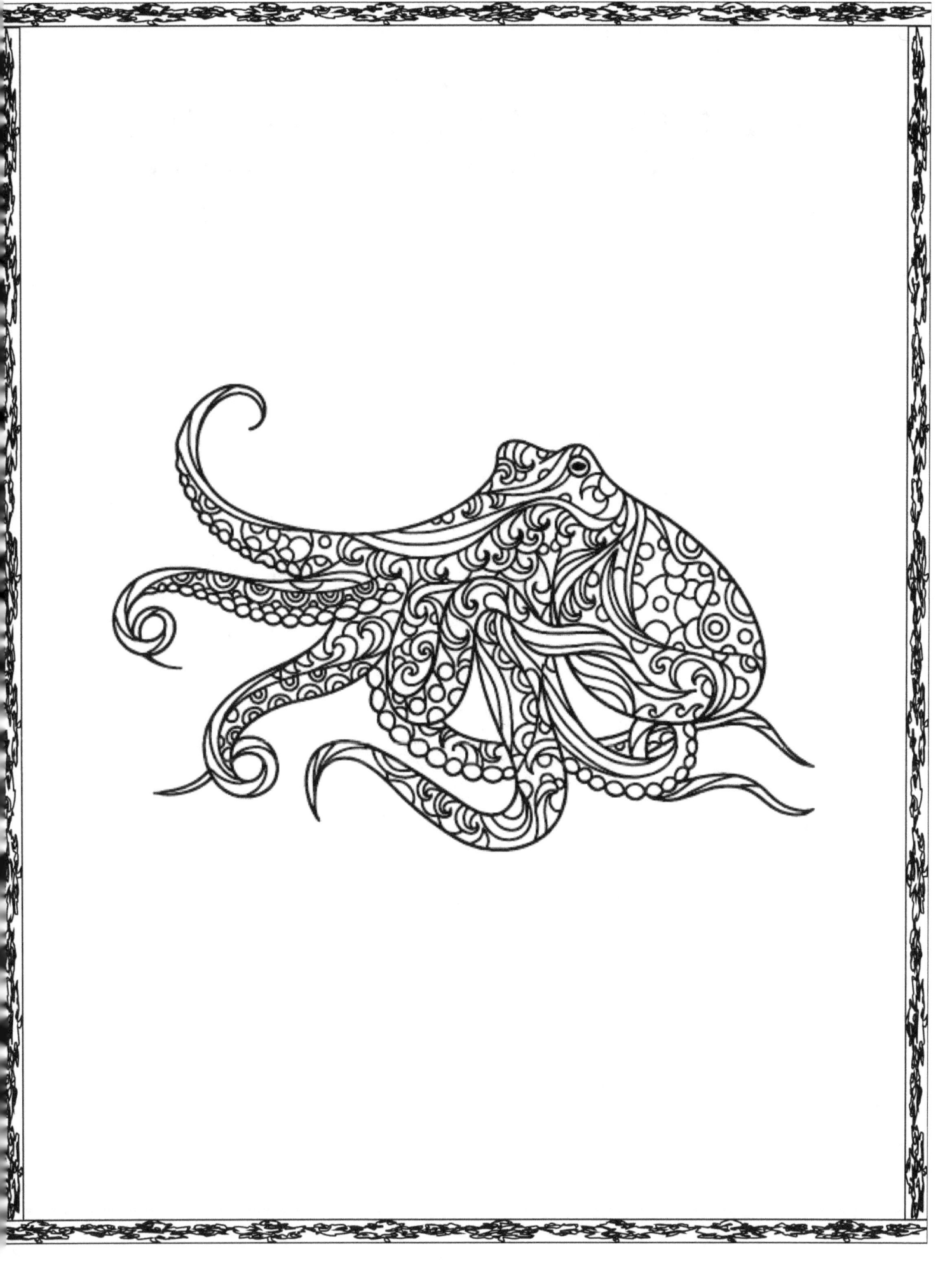

TEST YOUR COLOR

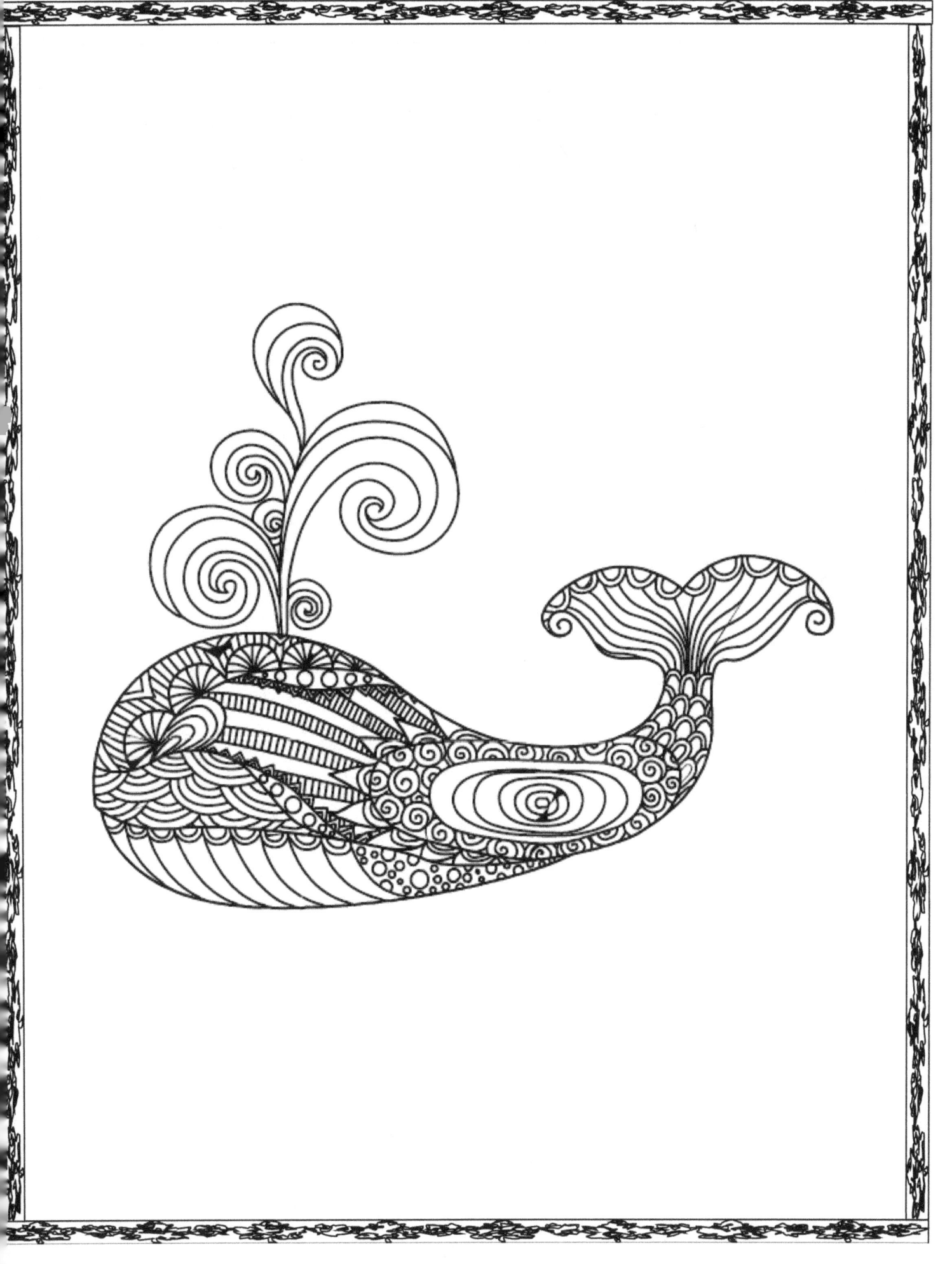

TEST YOUR COLOR

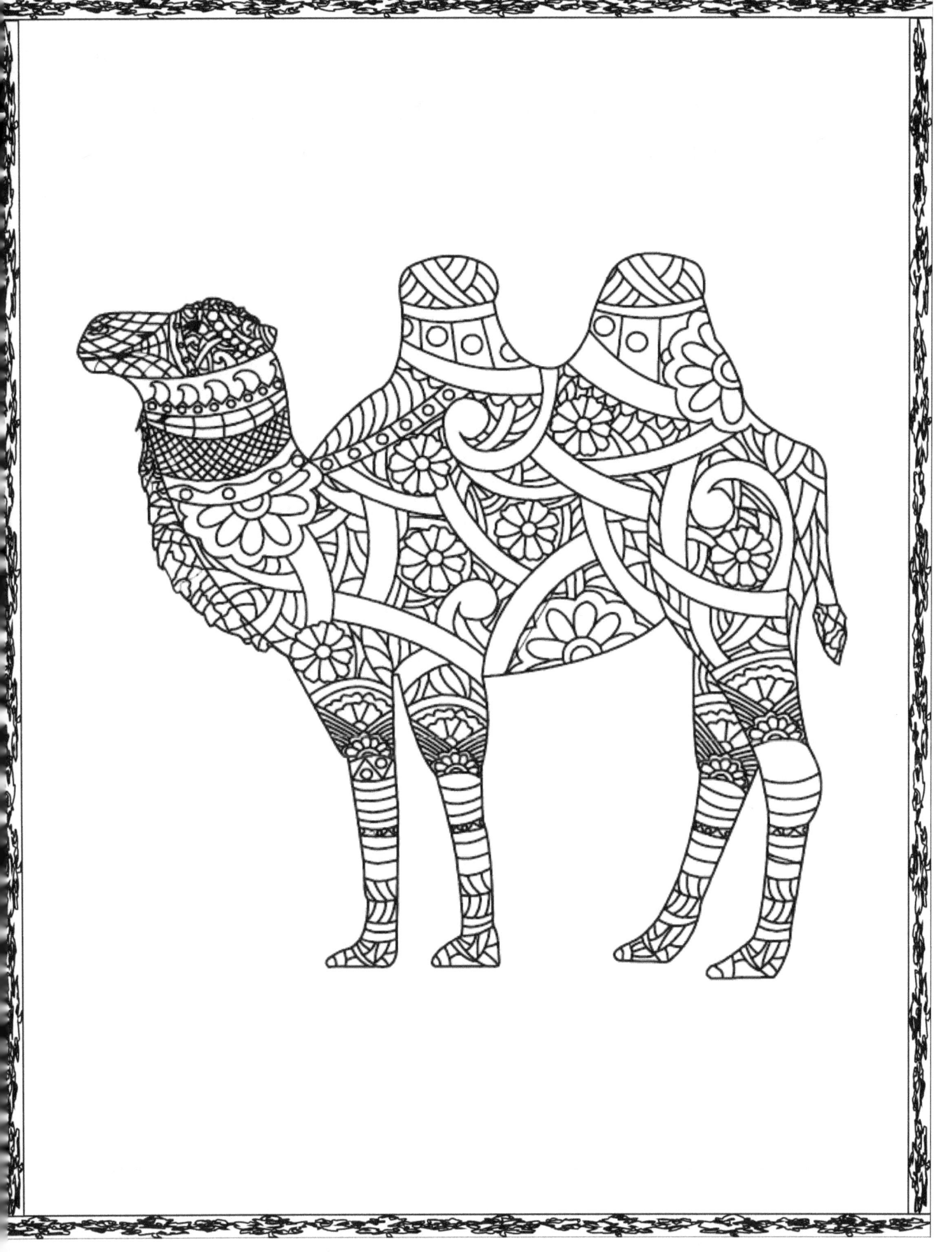

TEST YOUR COLOR

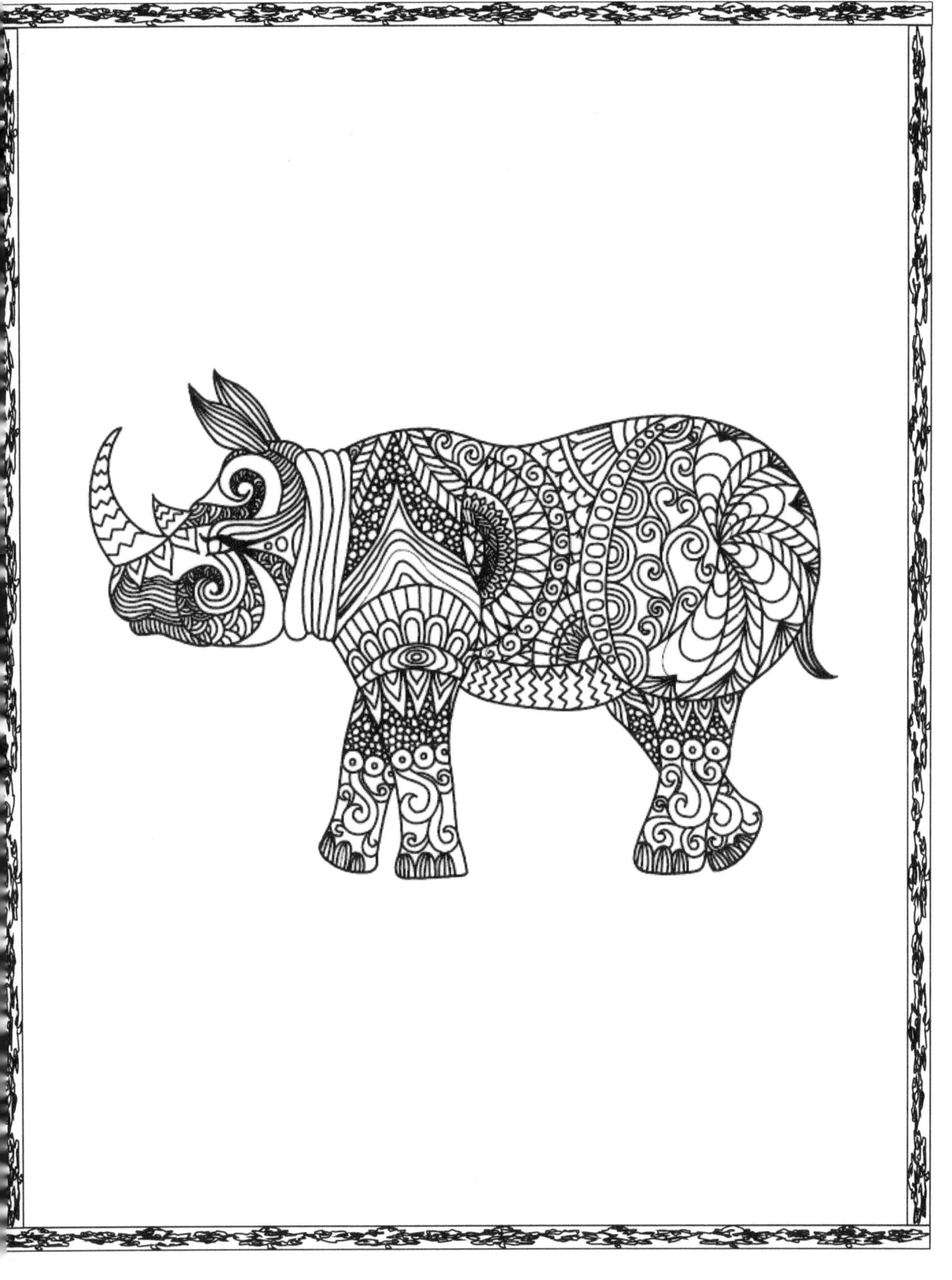

TEST YOUR COLOR

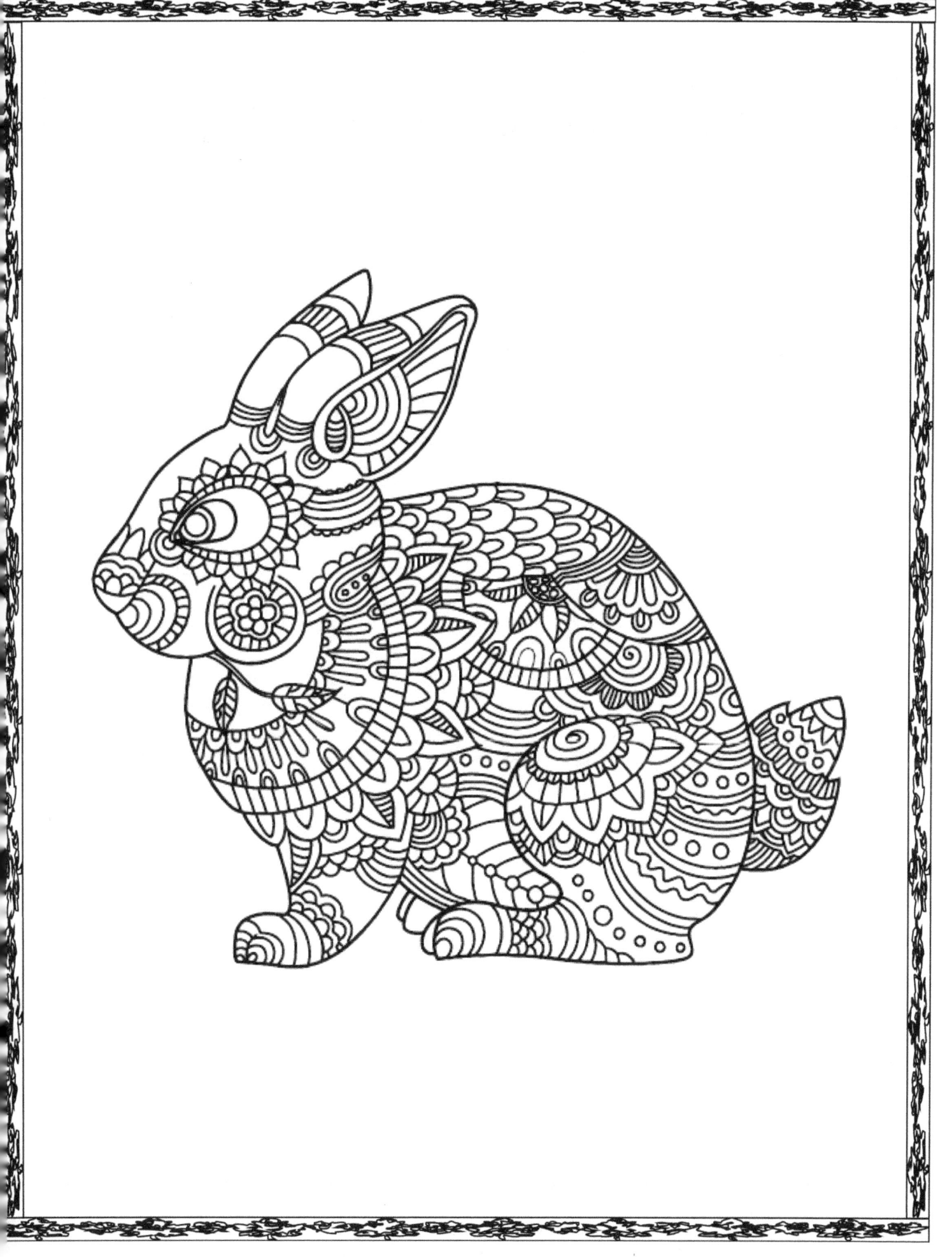

TEST YOUR COLOR

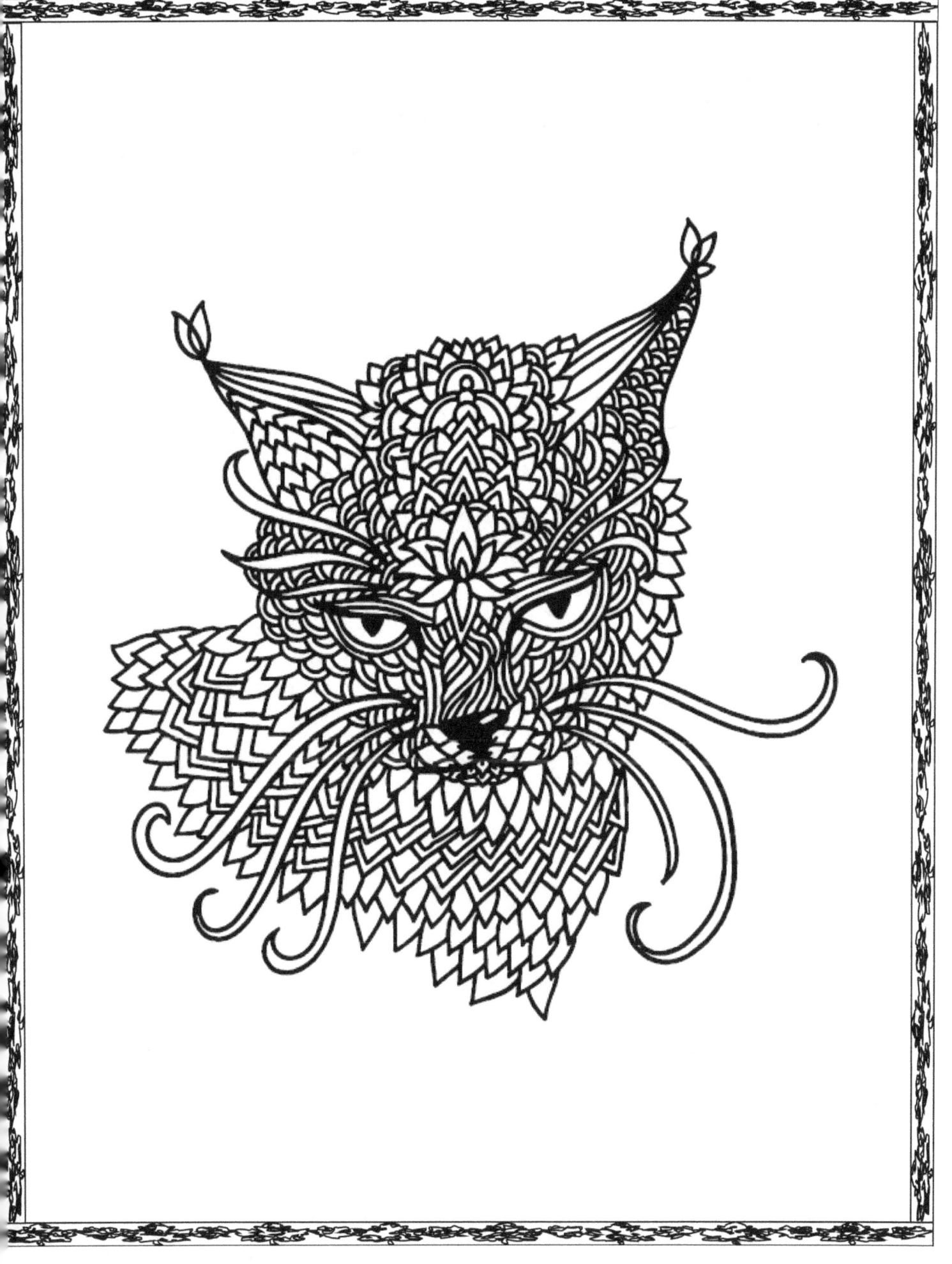

TEST YOUR COLOR

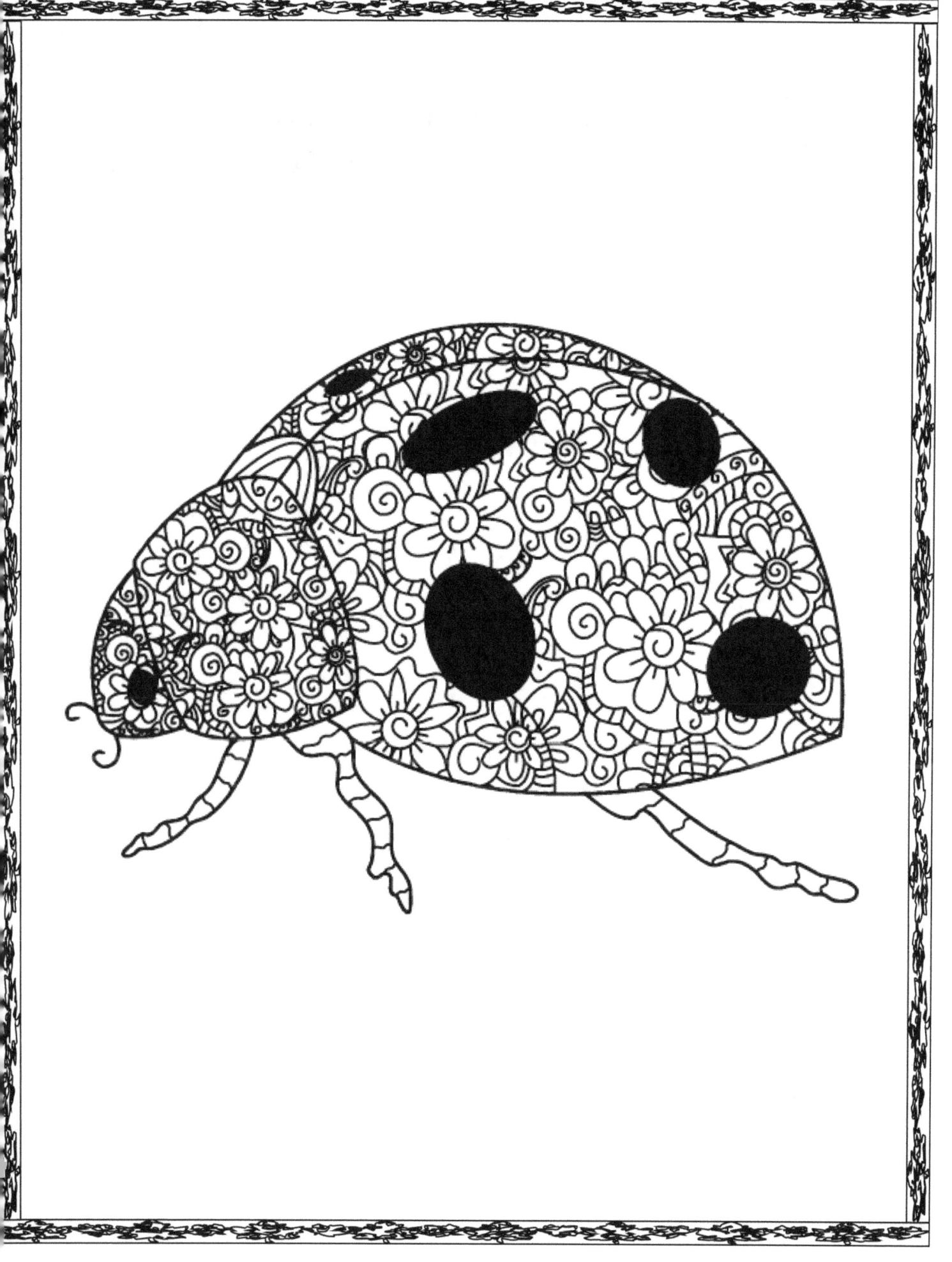

TEST YOUR COLOR

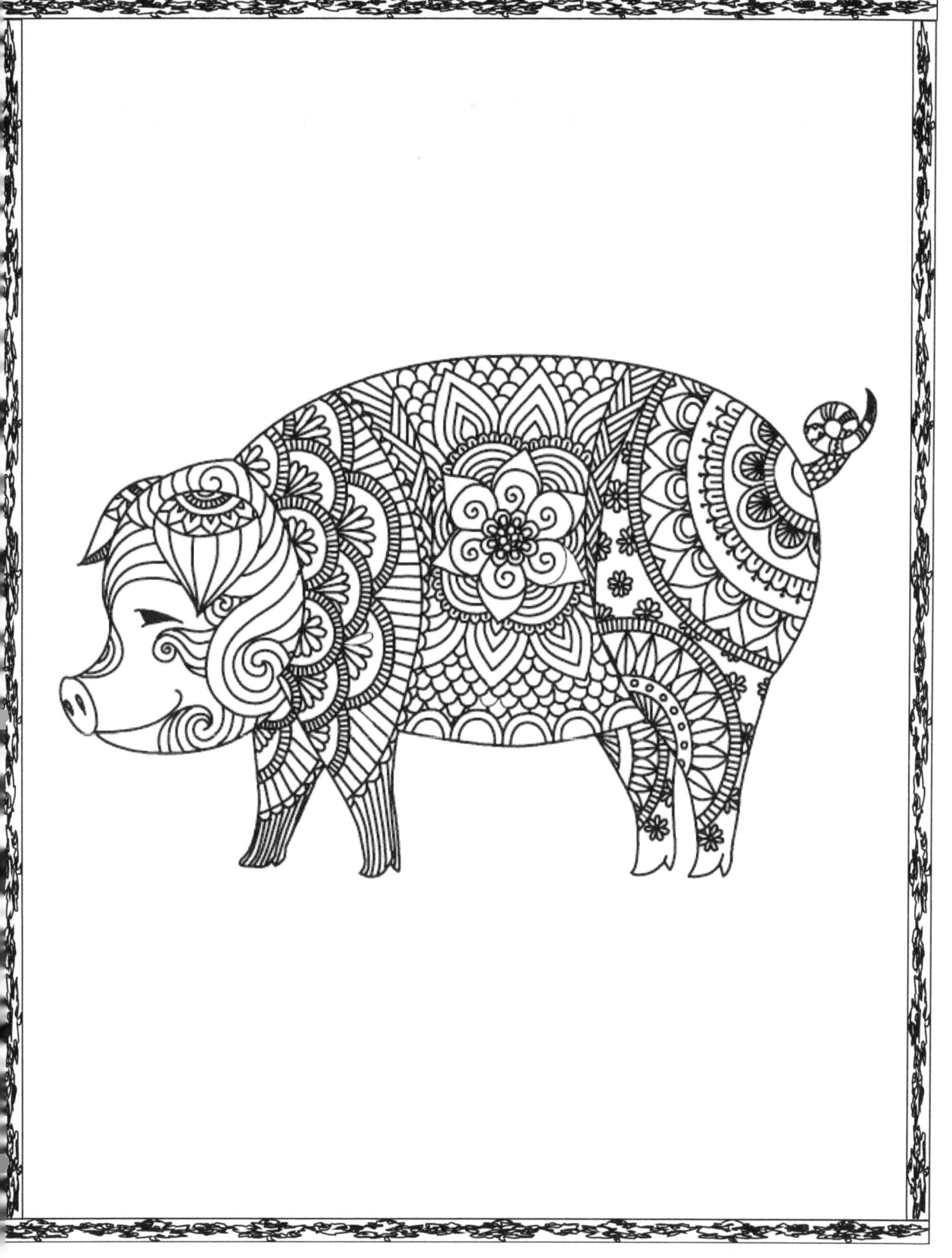

TEST YOUR COLOR

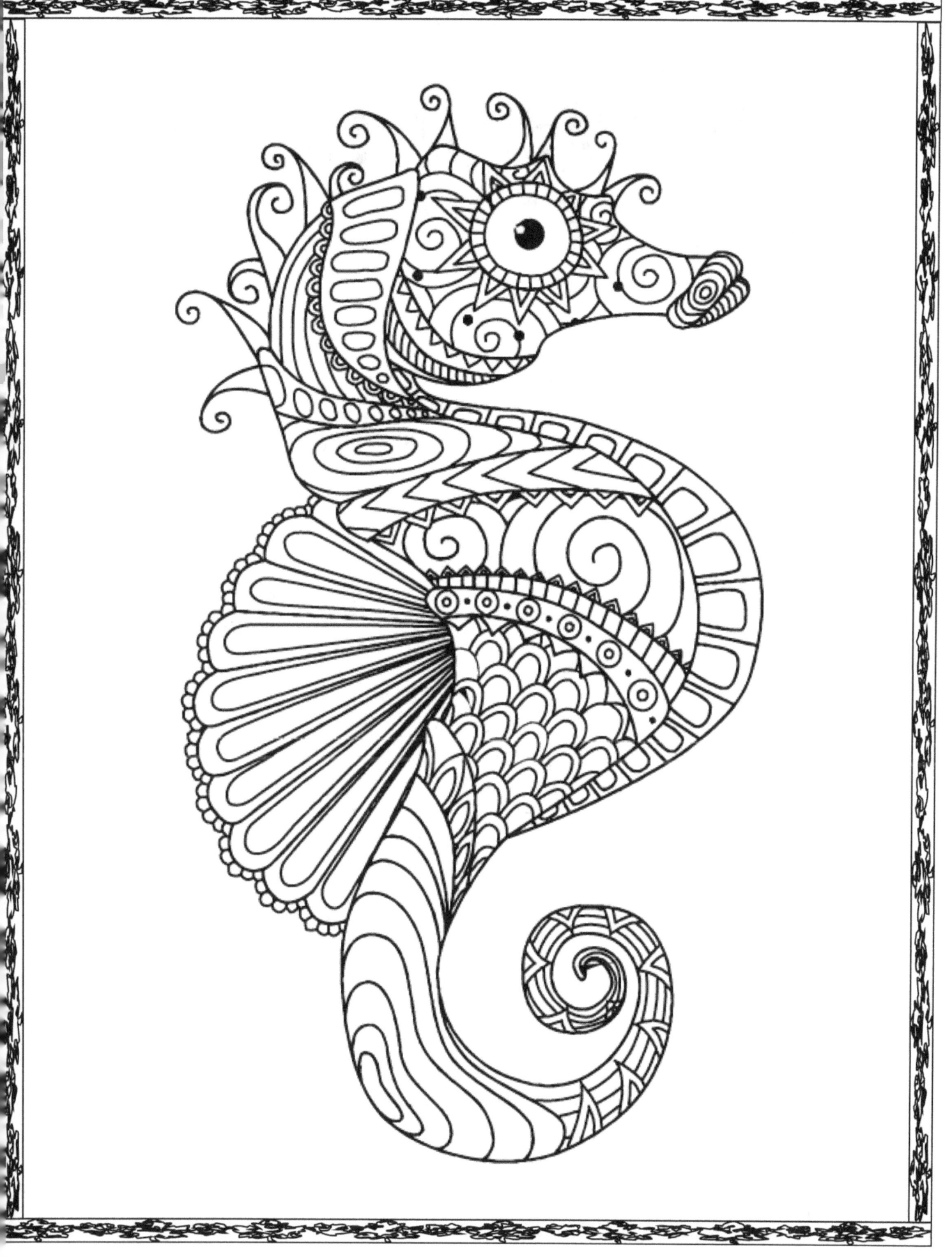

TEST YOUR COLOR

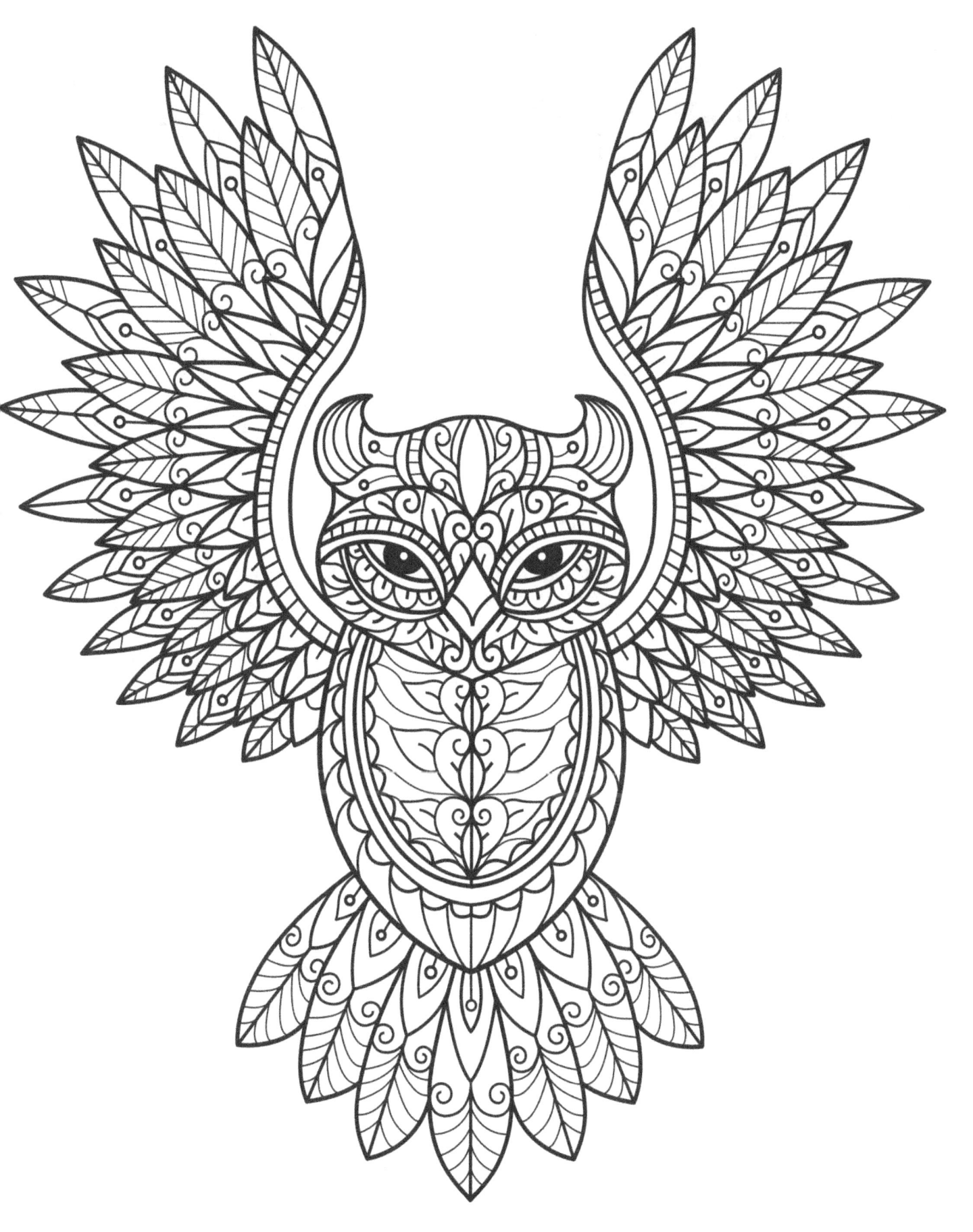

TEST YOUR COLOR

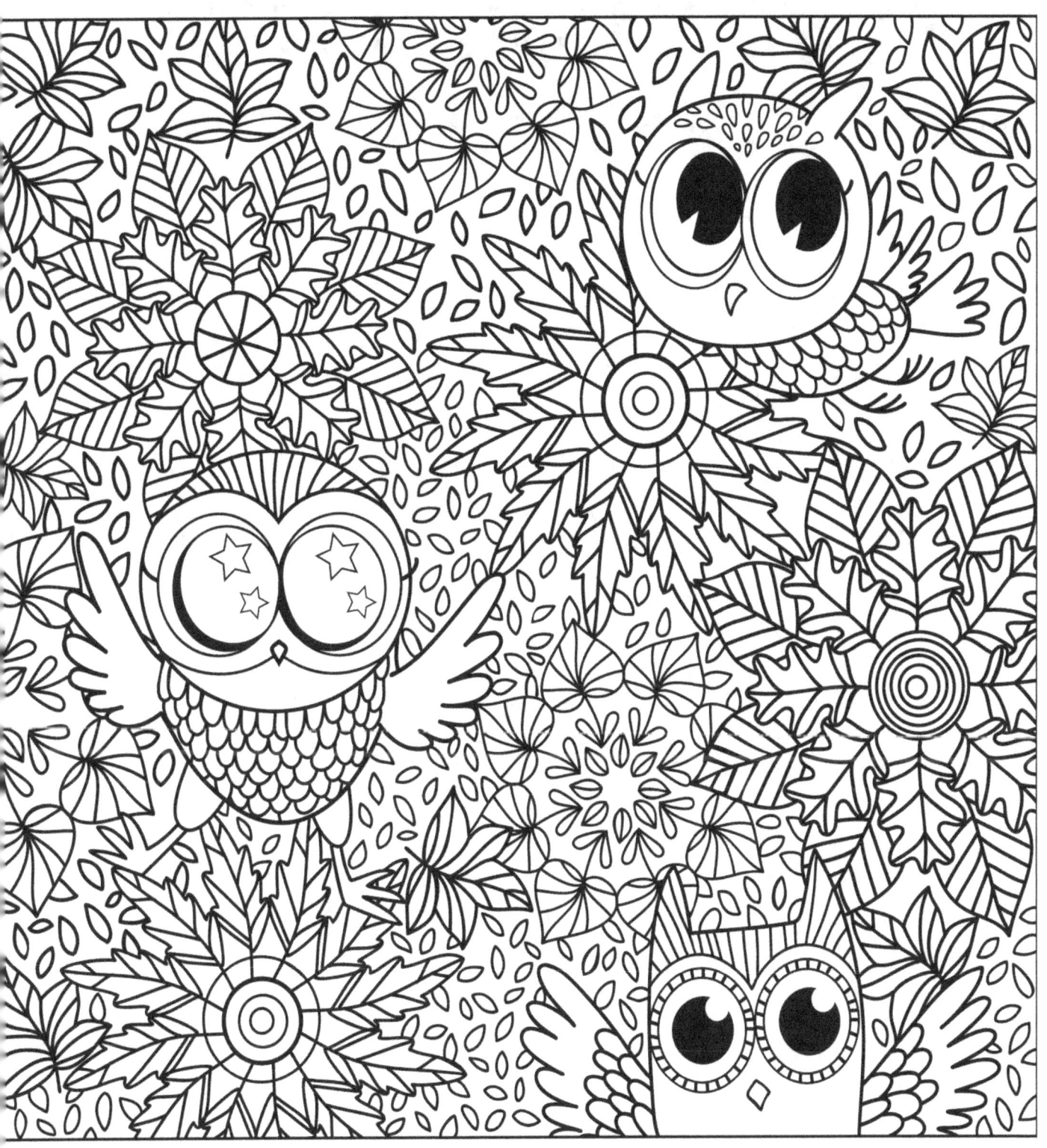

TEST YOUR COLOR

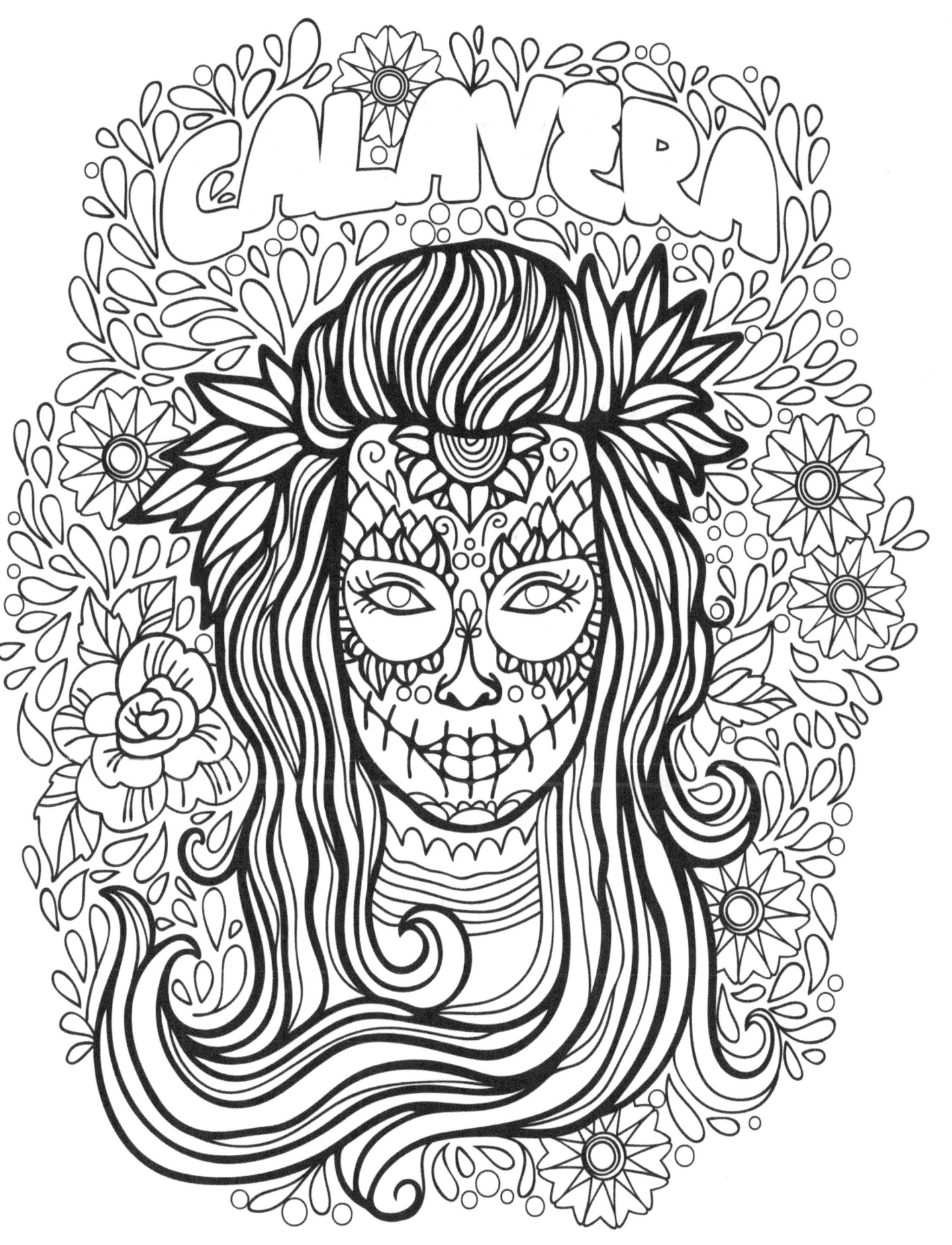

TEST YOUR COLOR

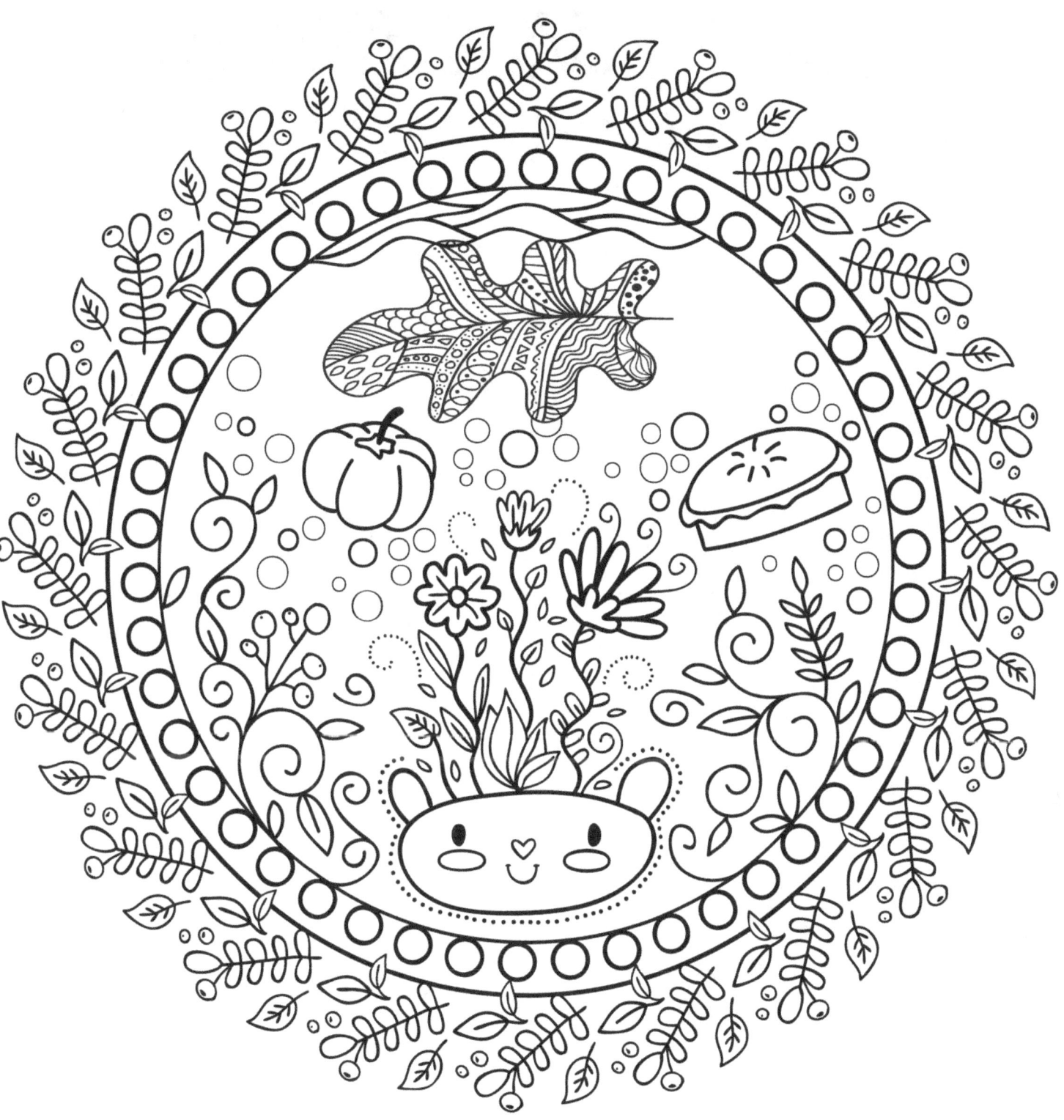

TEST YOUR COLOR

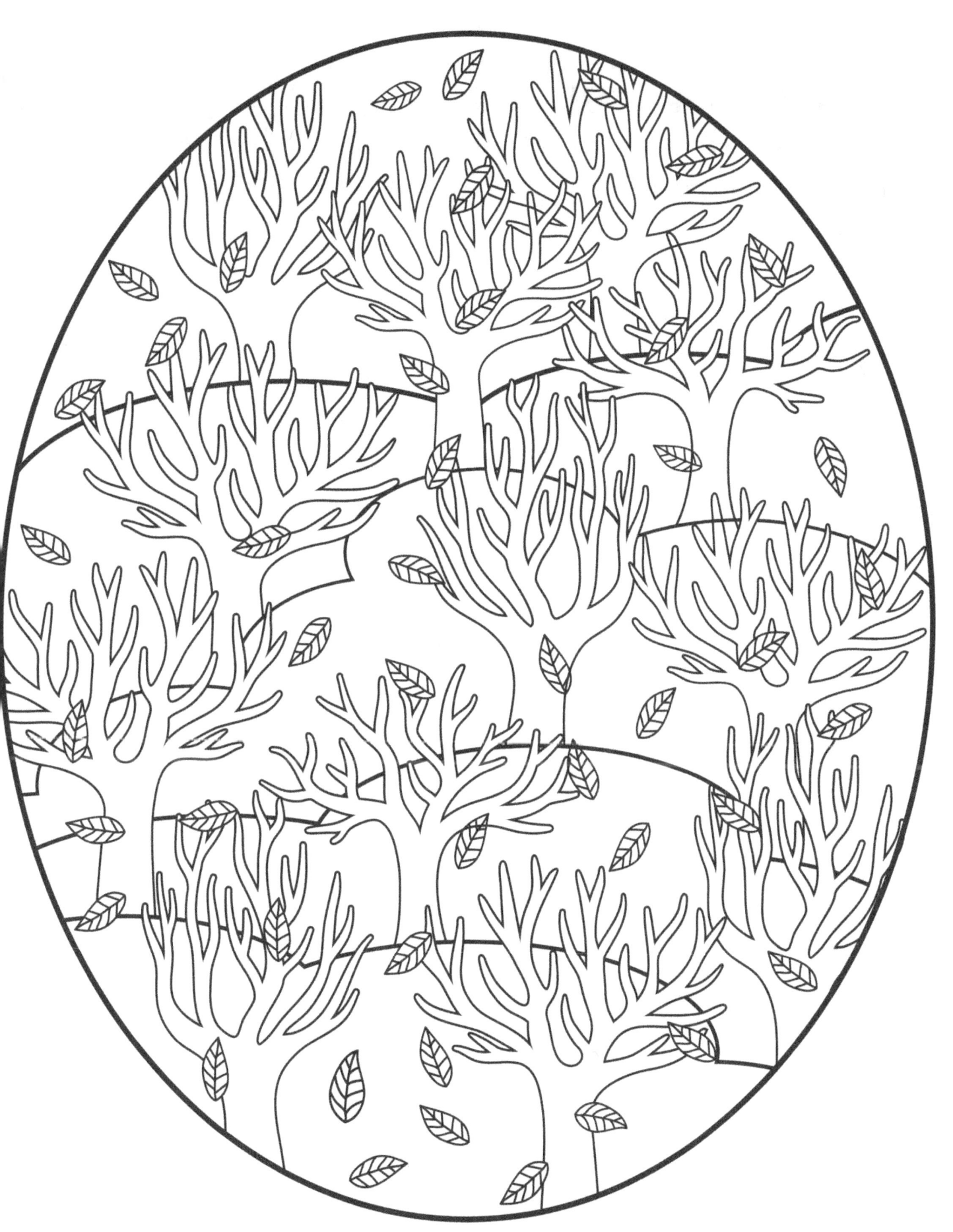

TEST YOUR COLOR

TEST YOUR COLOR

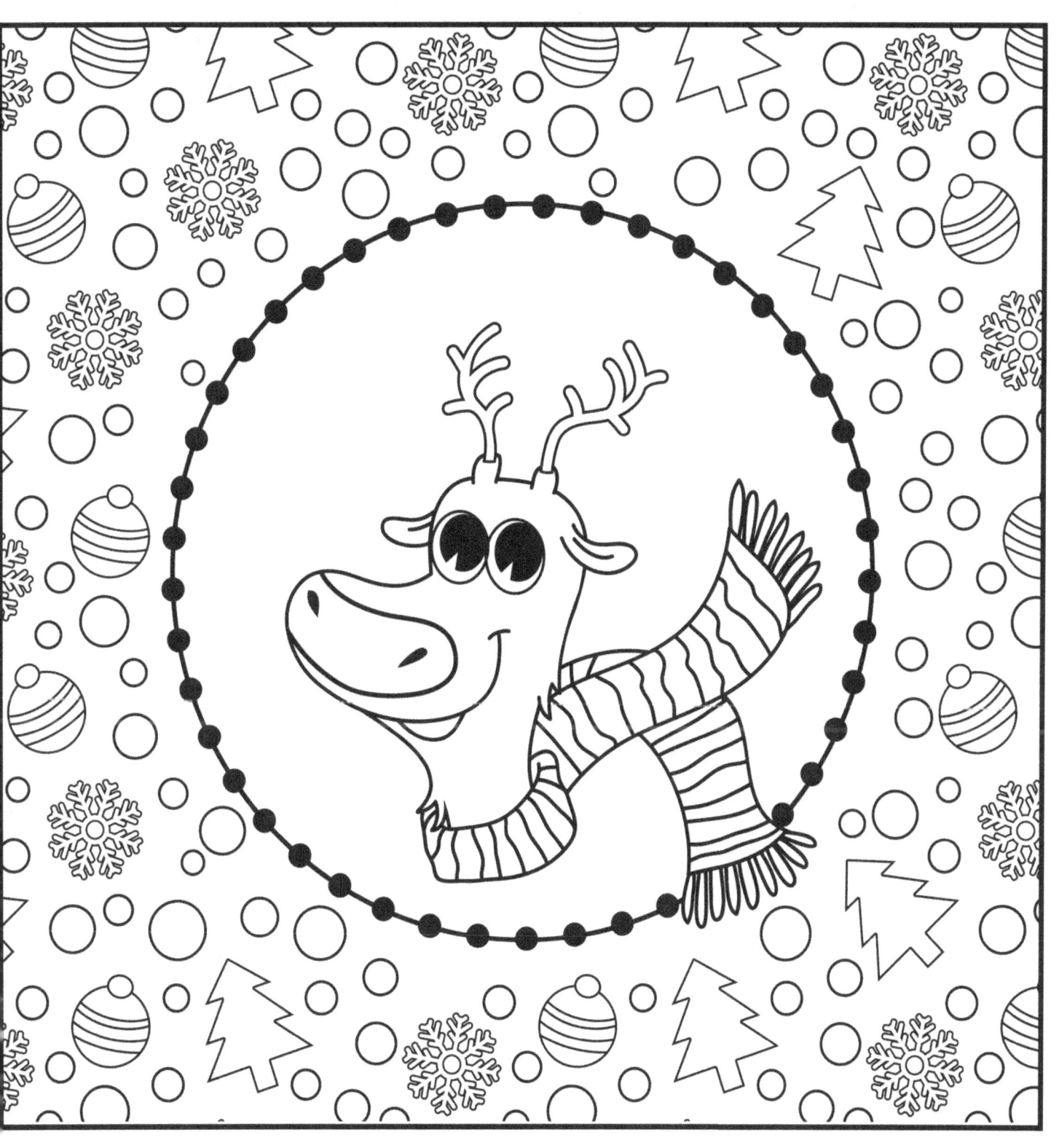

TEST YOUR COLOR

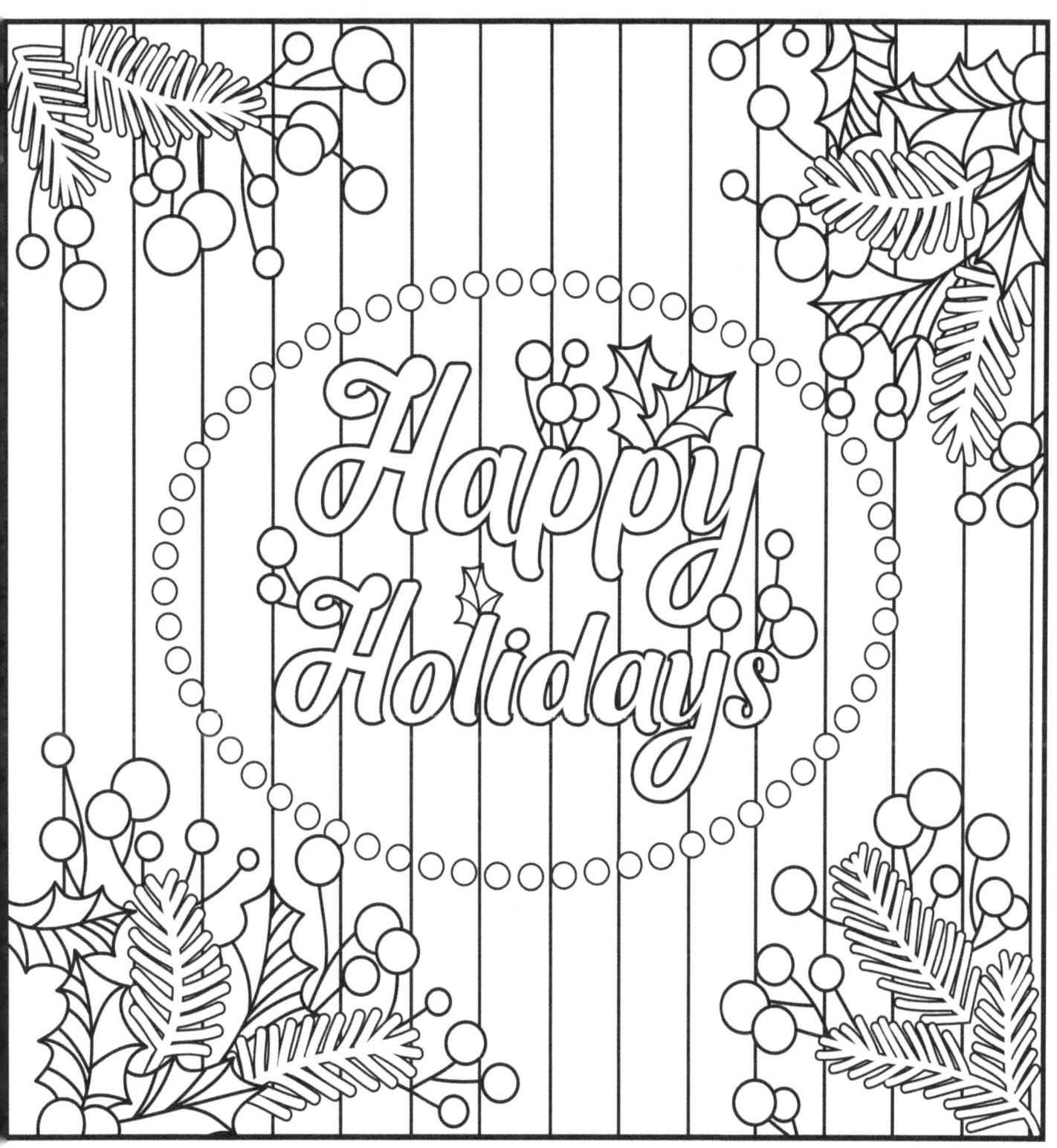

TEST YOUR COLOR

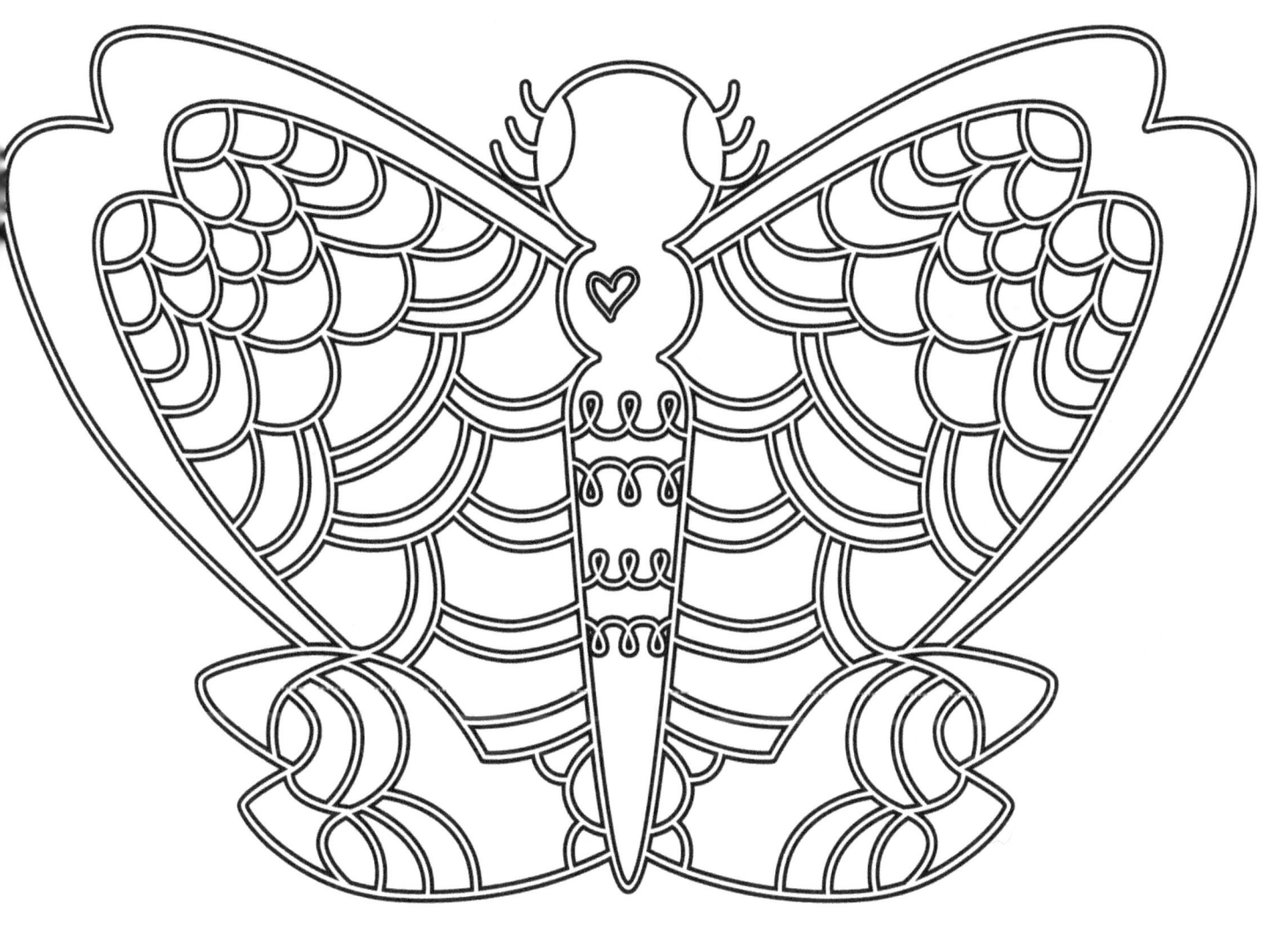

TEST YOUR COLOR

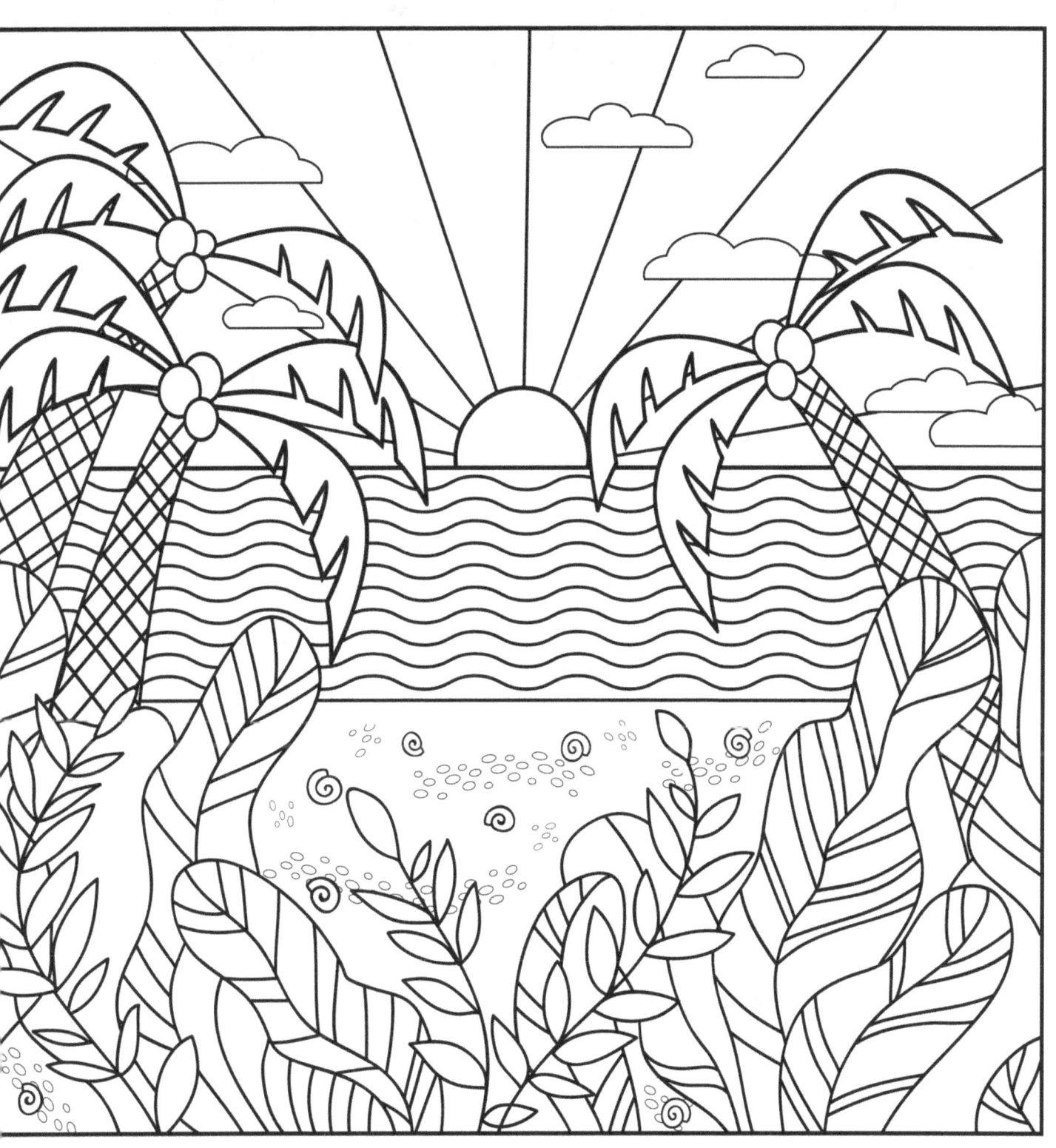

TEST YOUR COLOR

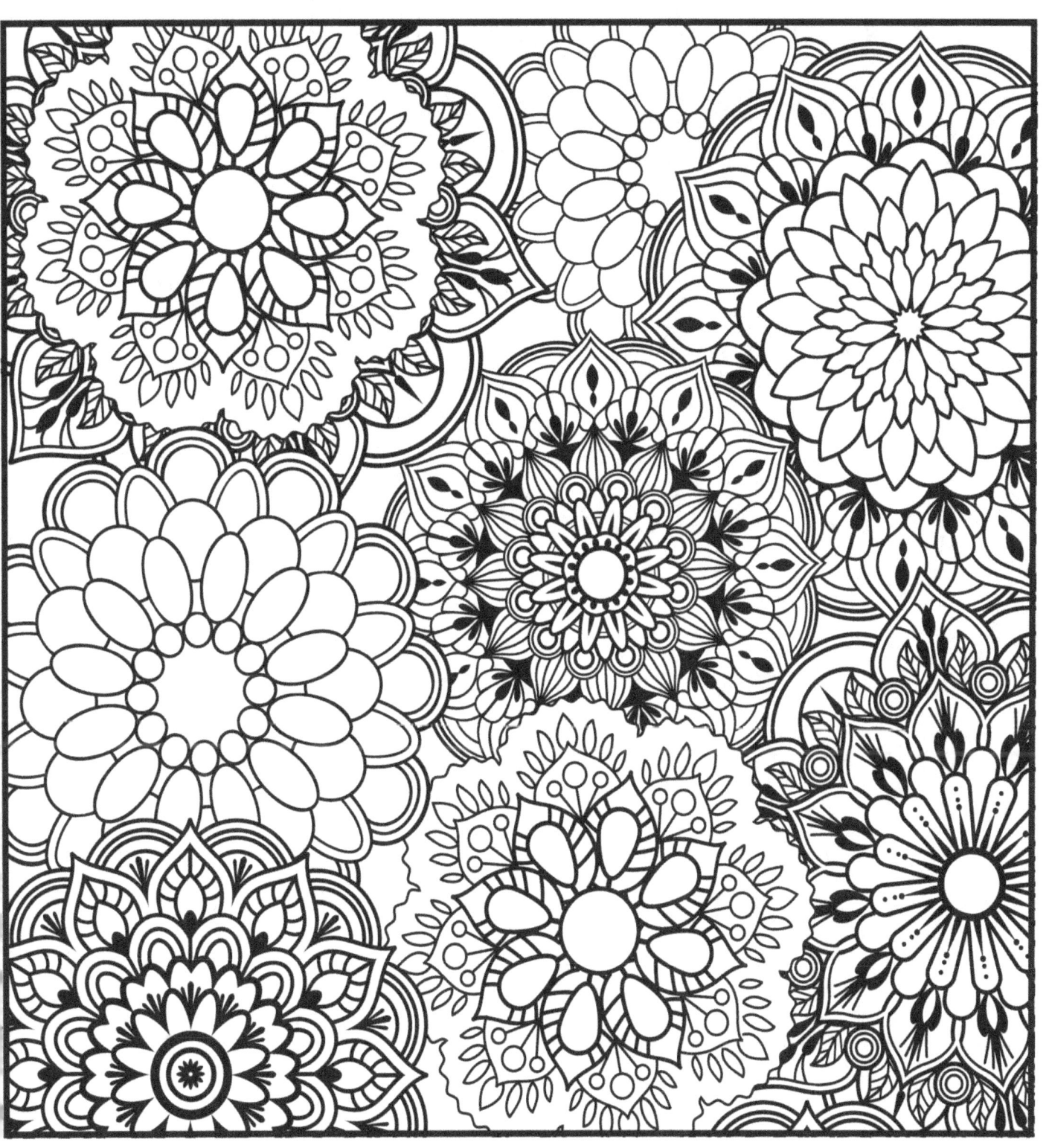

TEST YOUR COLOR

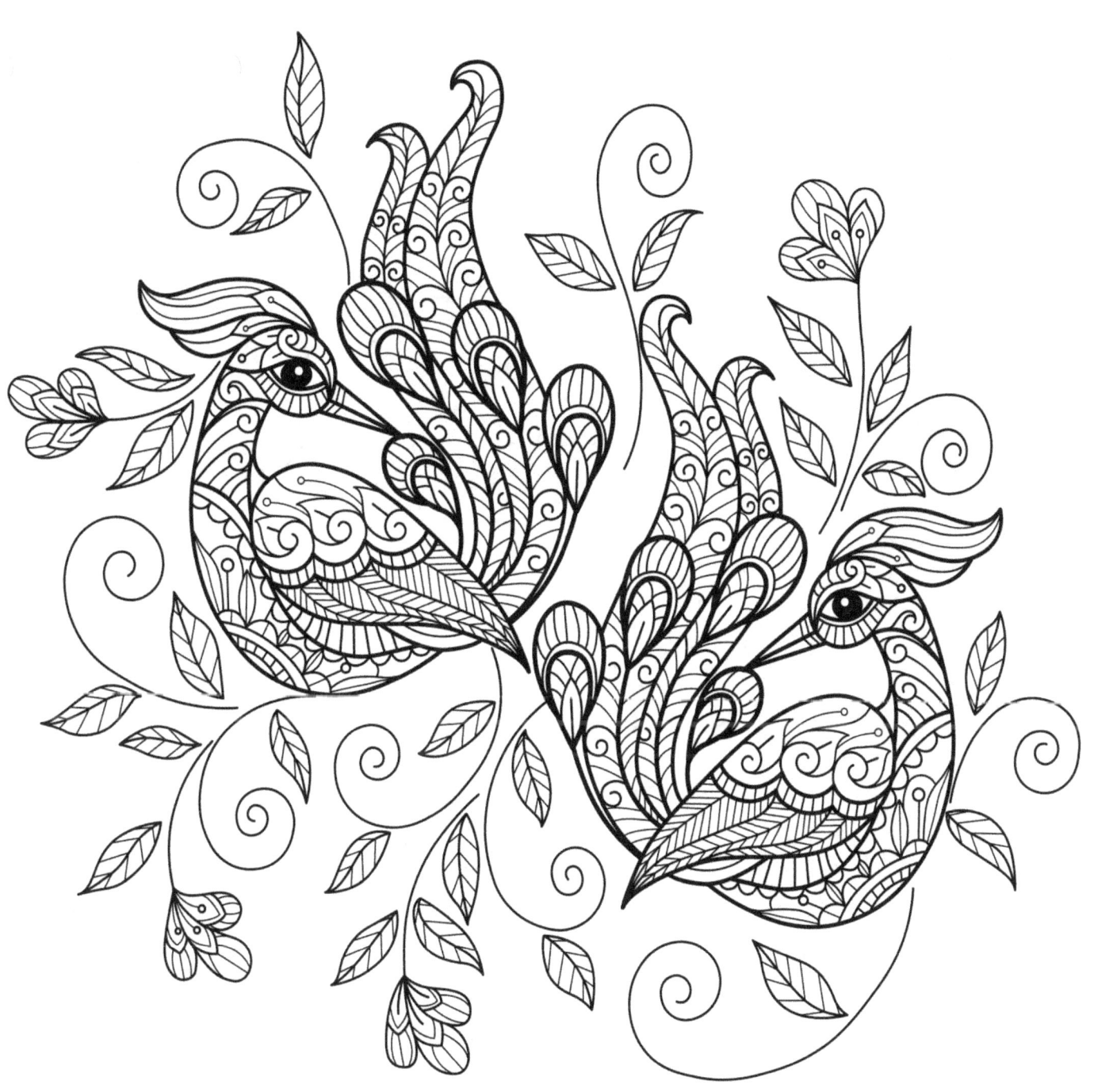

TEST YOUR COLOR

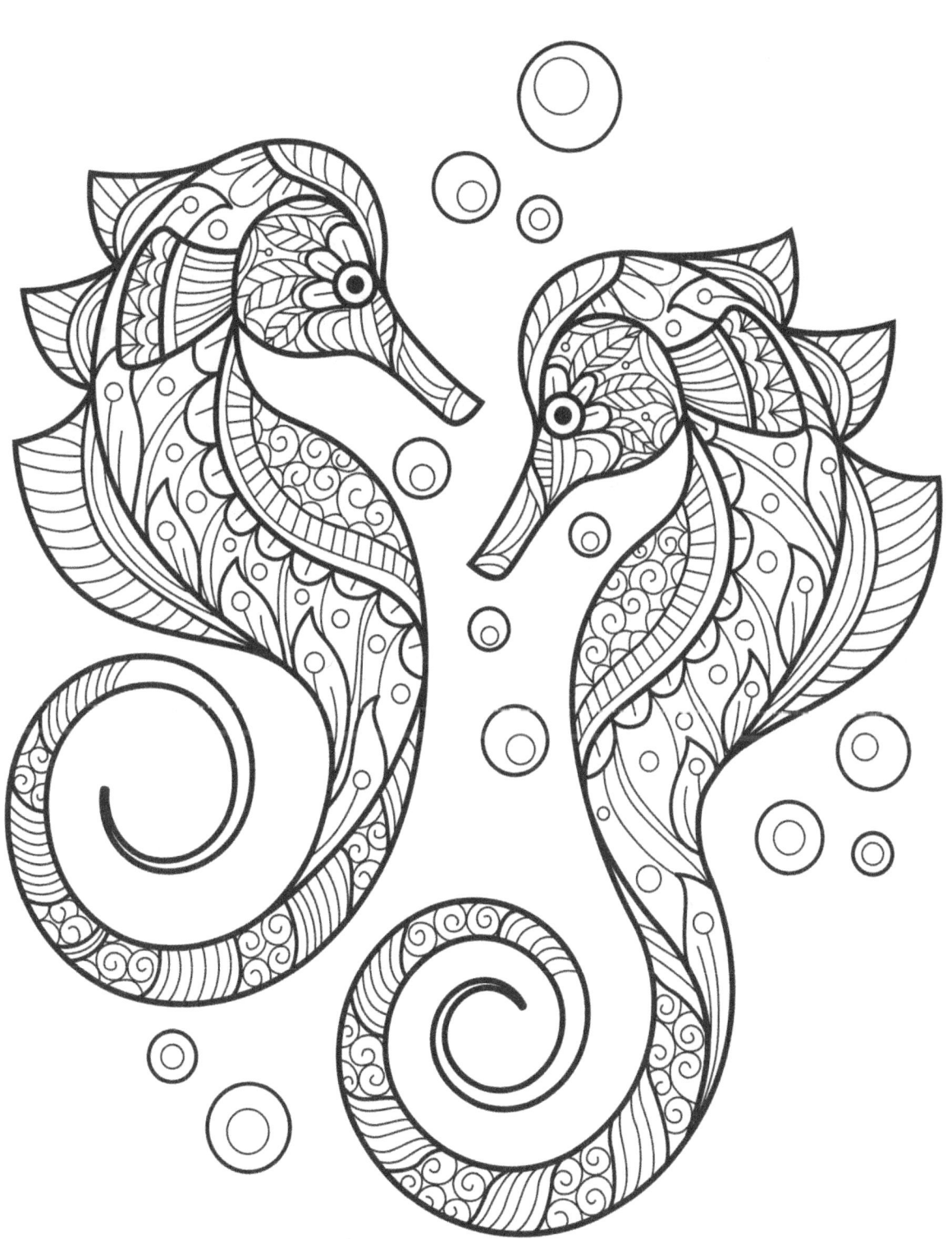

TEST YOUR COLOR

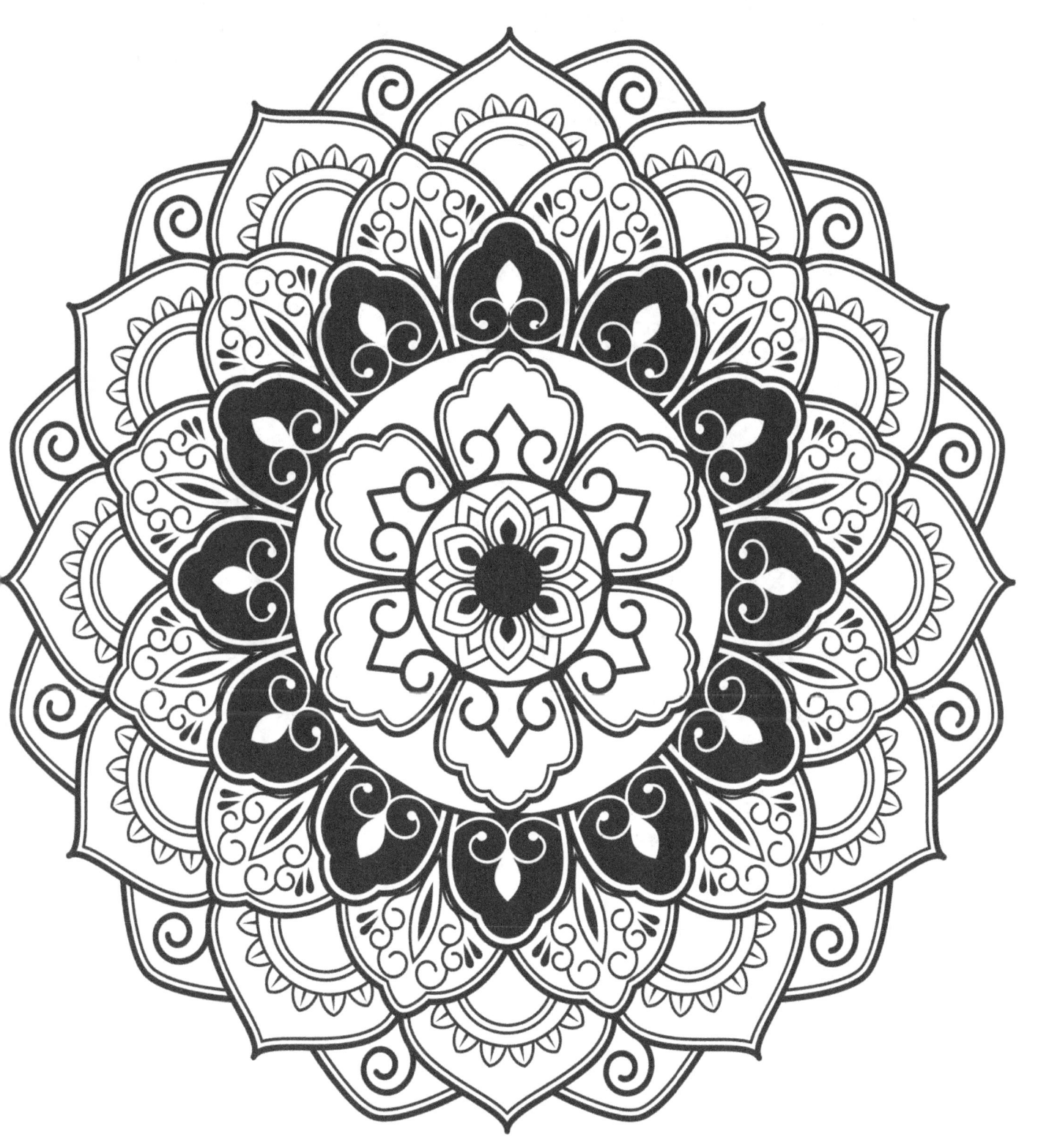

TEST YOUR COLOR

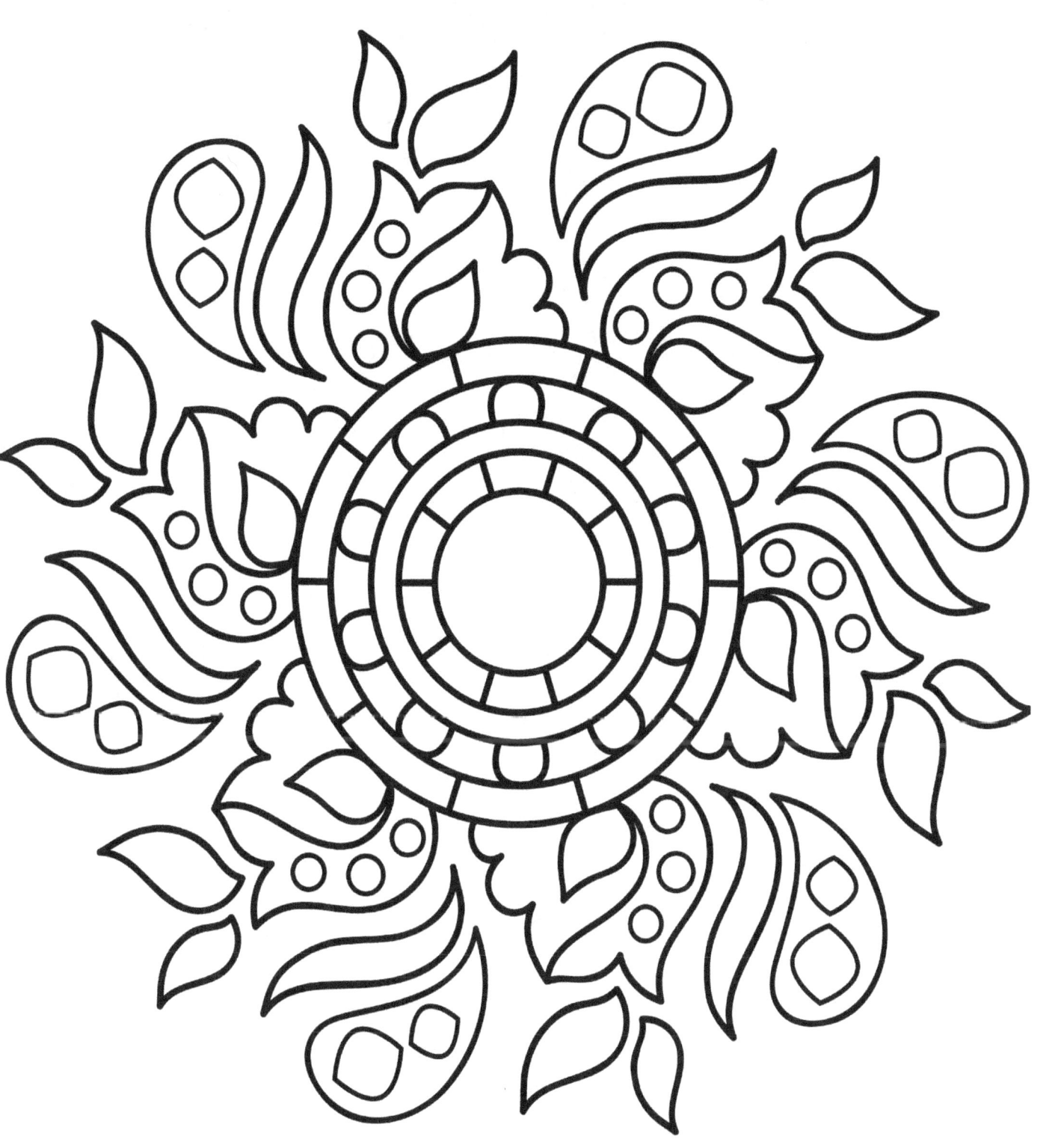

TEST YOUR COLOR

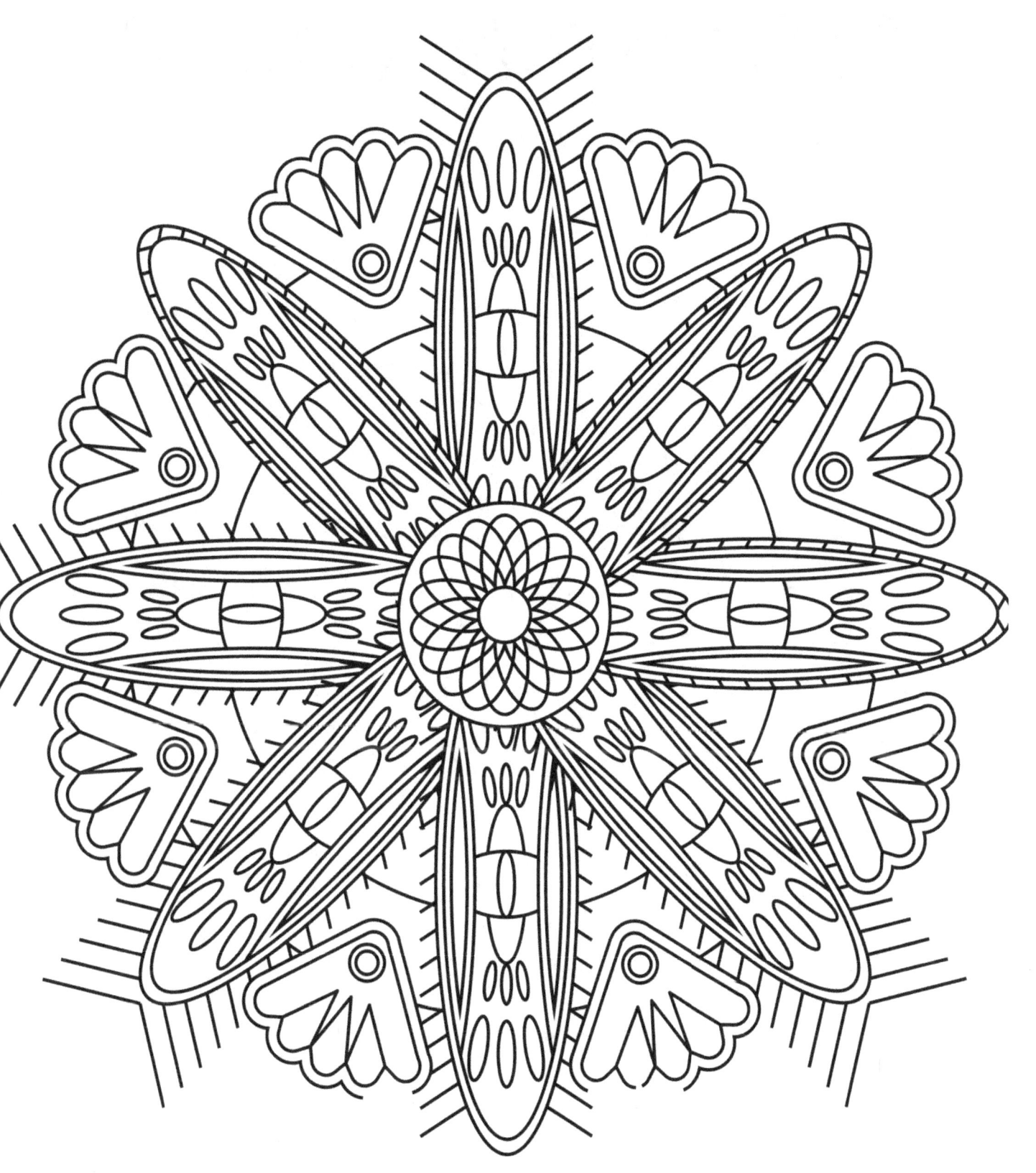

TEST YOUR COLOR

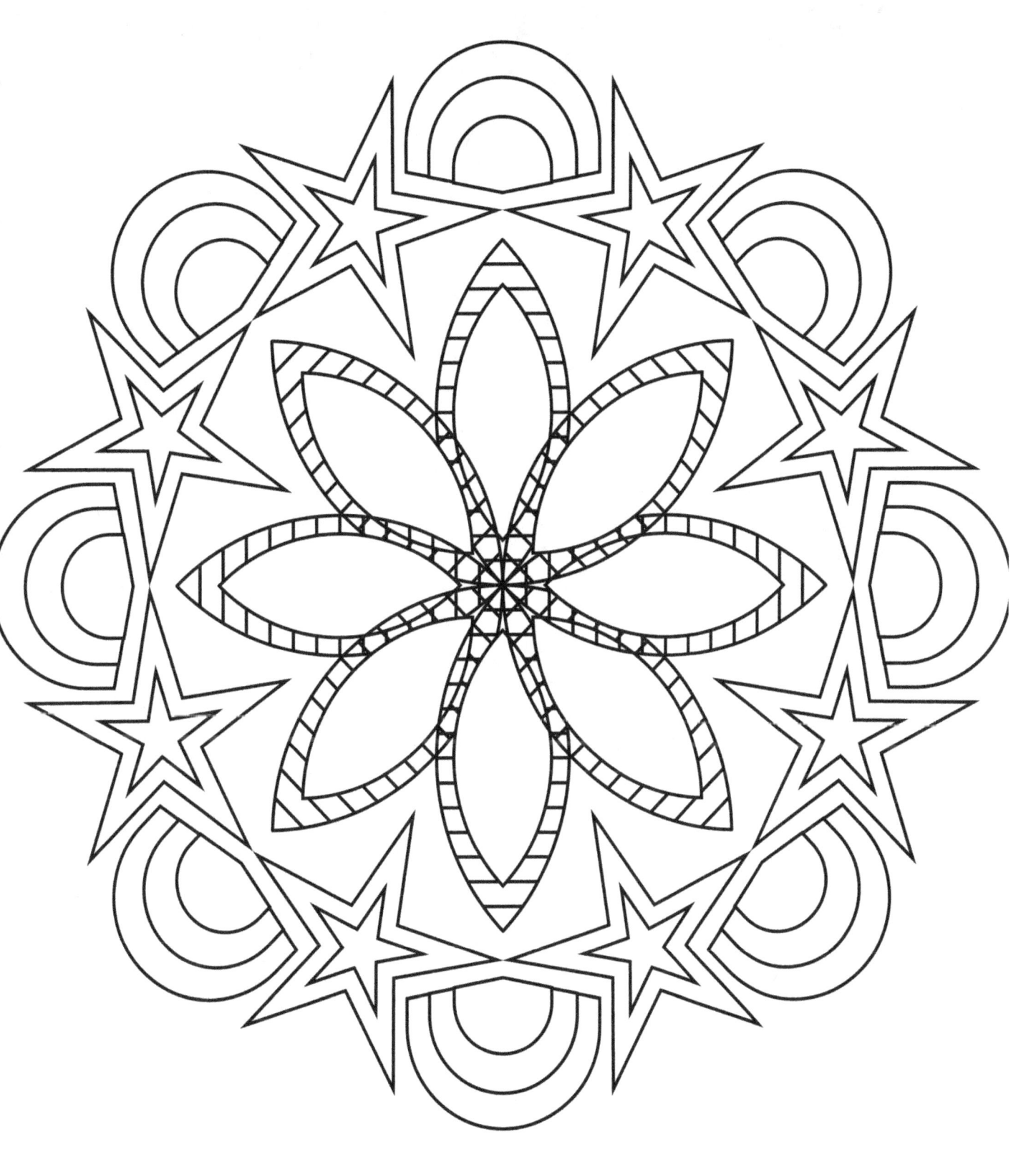

TEST YOUR COLOR

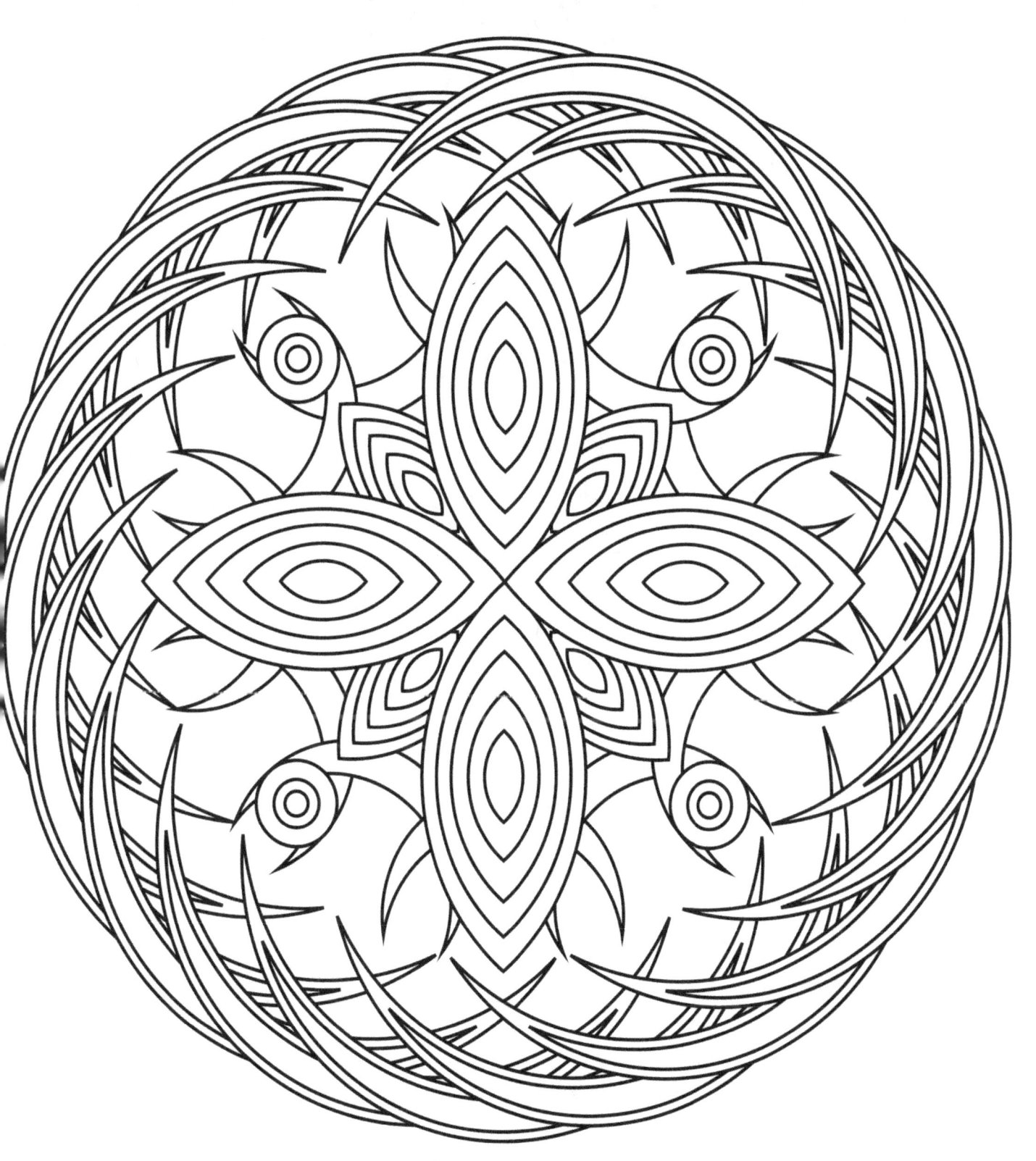

TEST YOUR COLOR

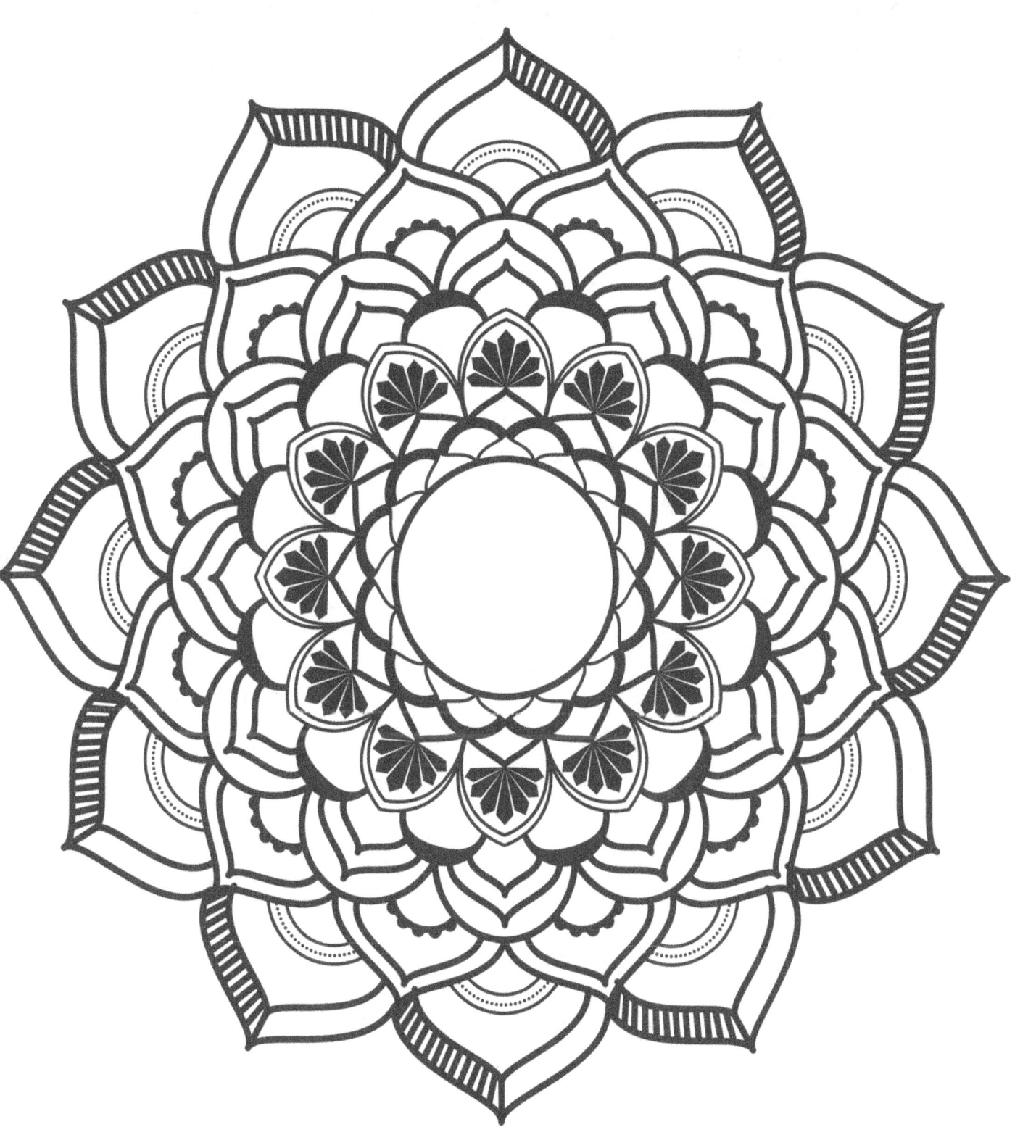

TEST YOUR COLOR

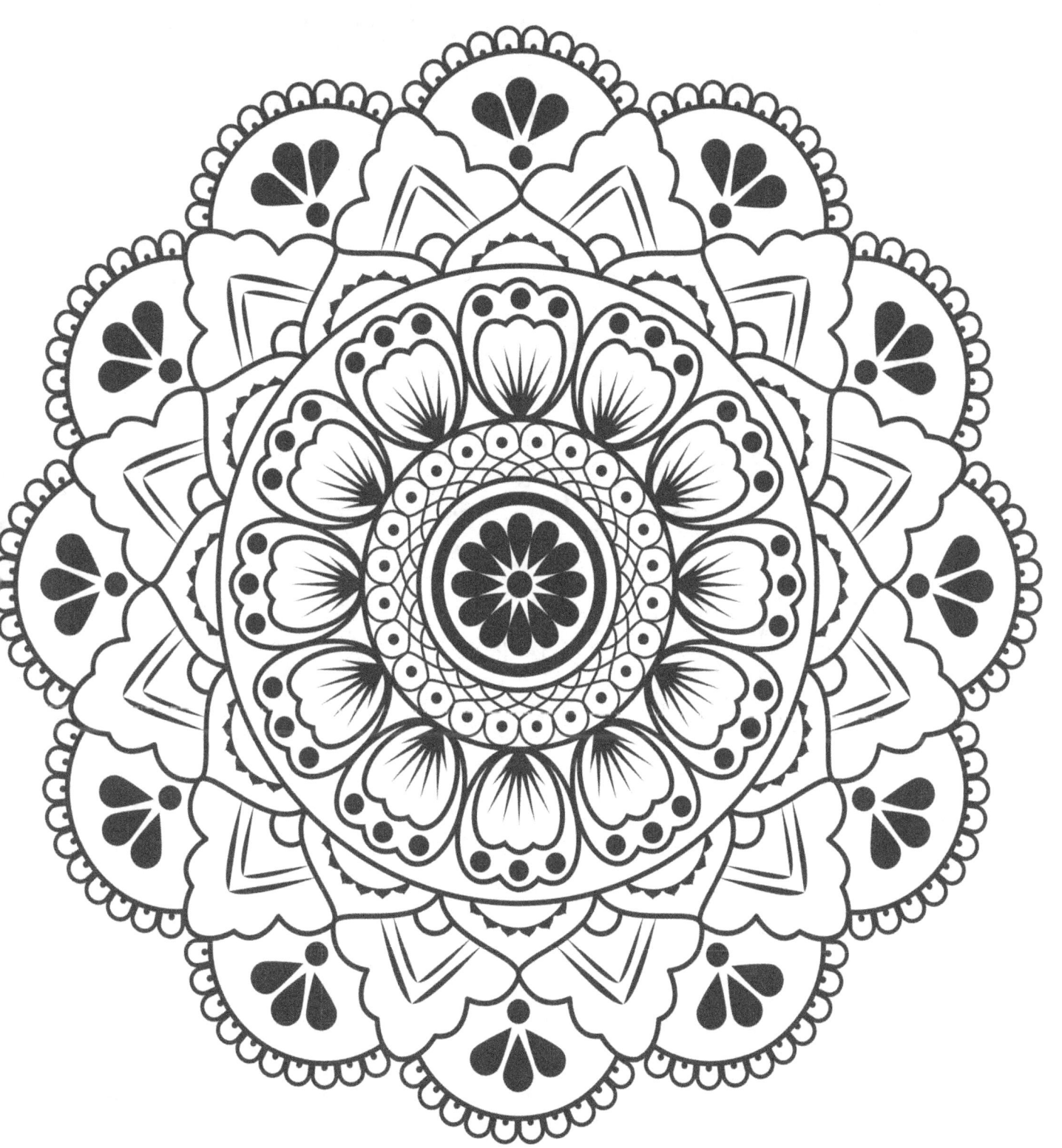

TEST YOUR COLOR

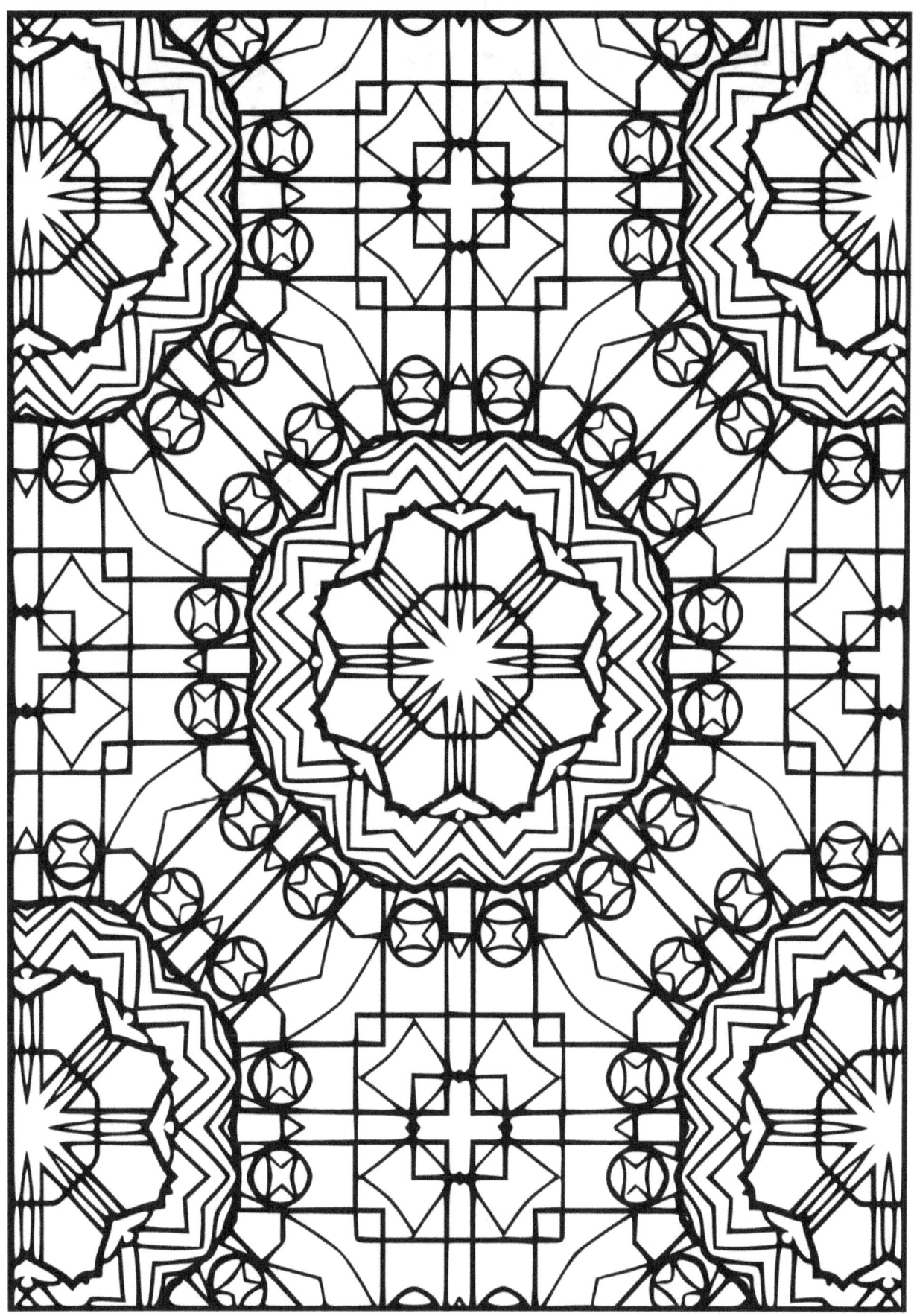

TEST YOUR COLOR

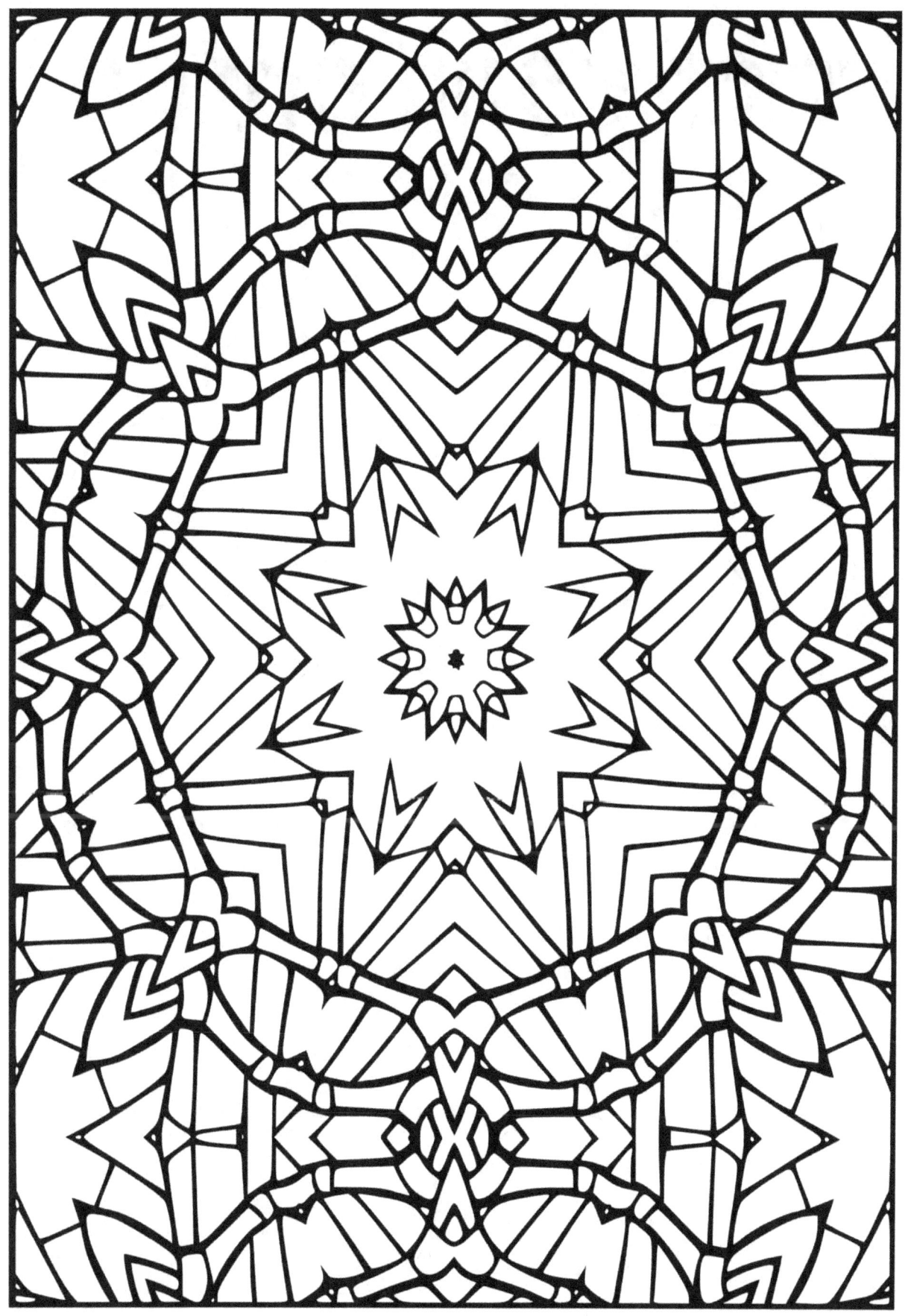

TEST YOUR COLOR

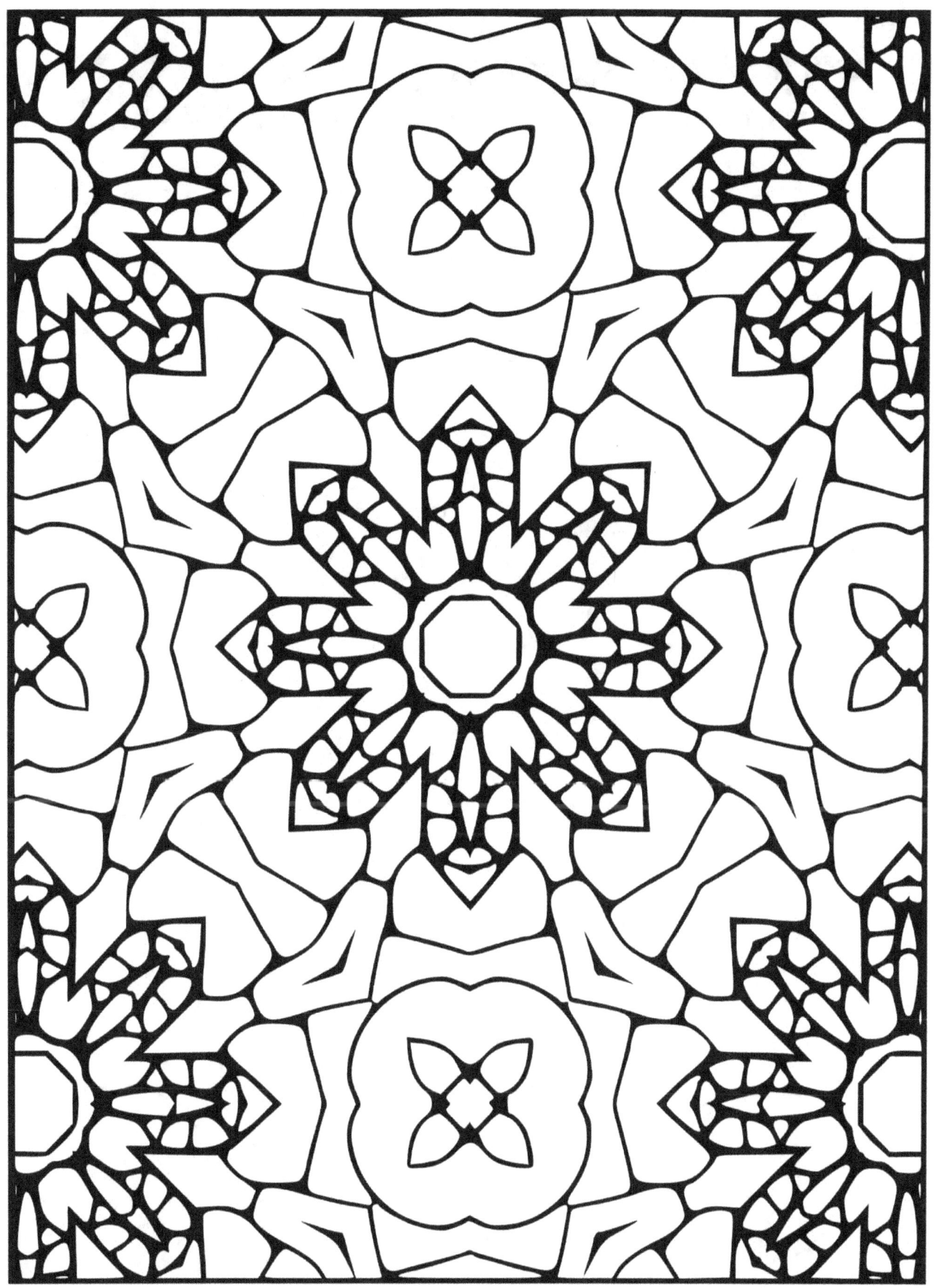

TEST YOUR COLOR

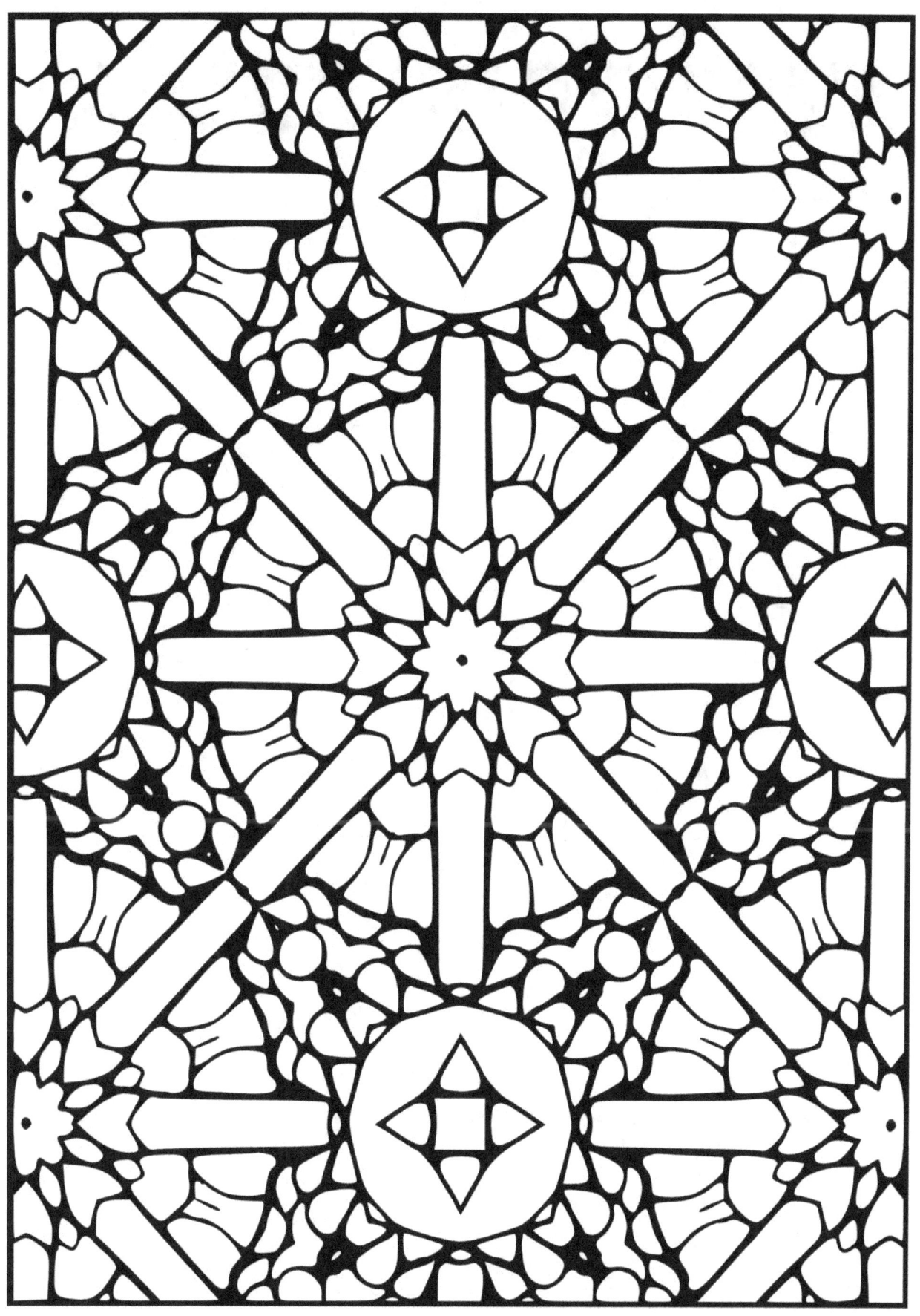

TEST YOUR COLOR

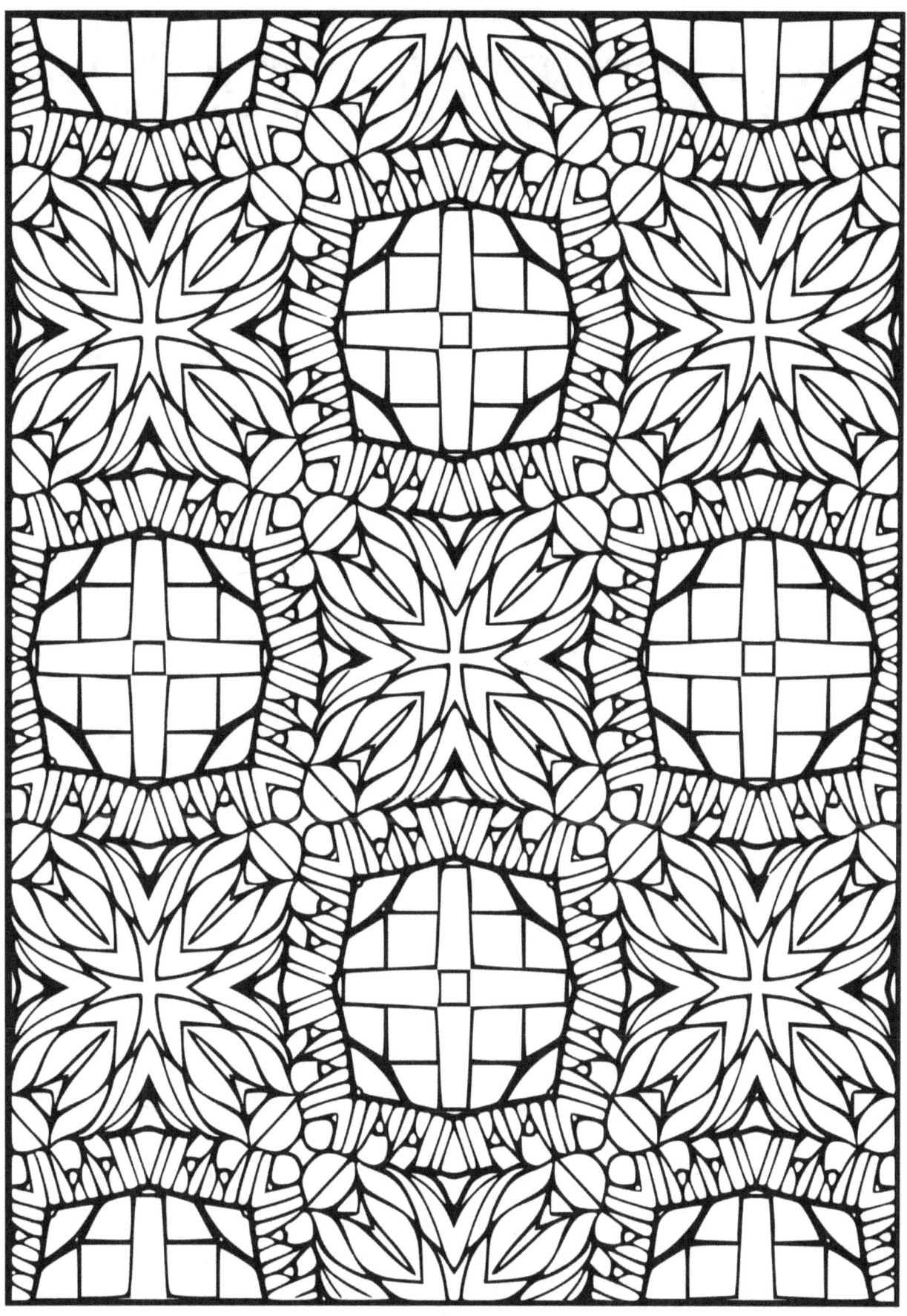

TEST YOUR COLOR

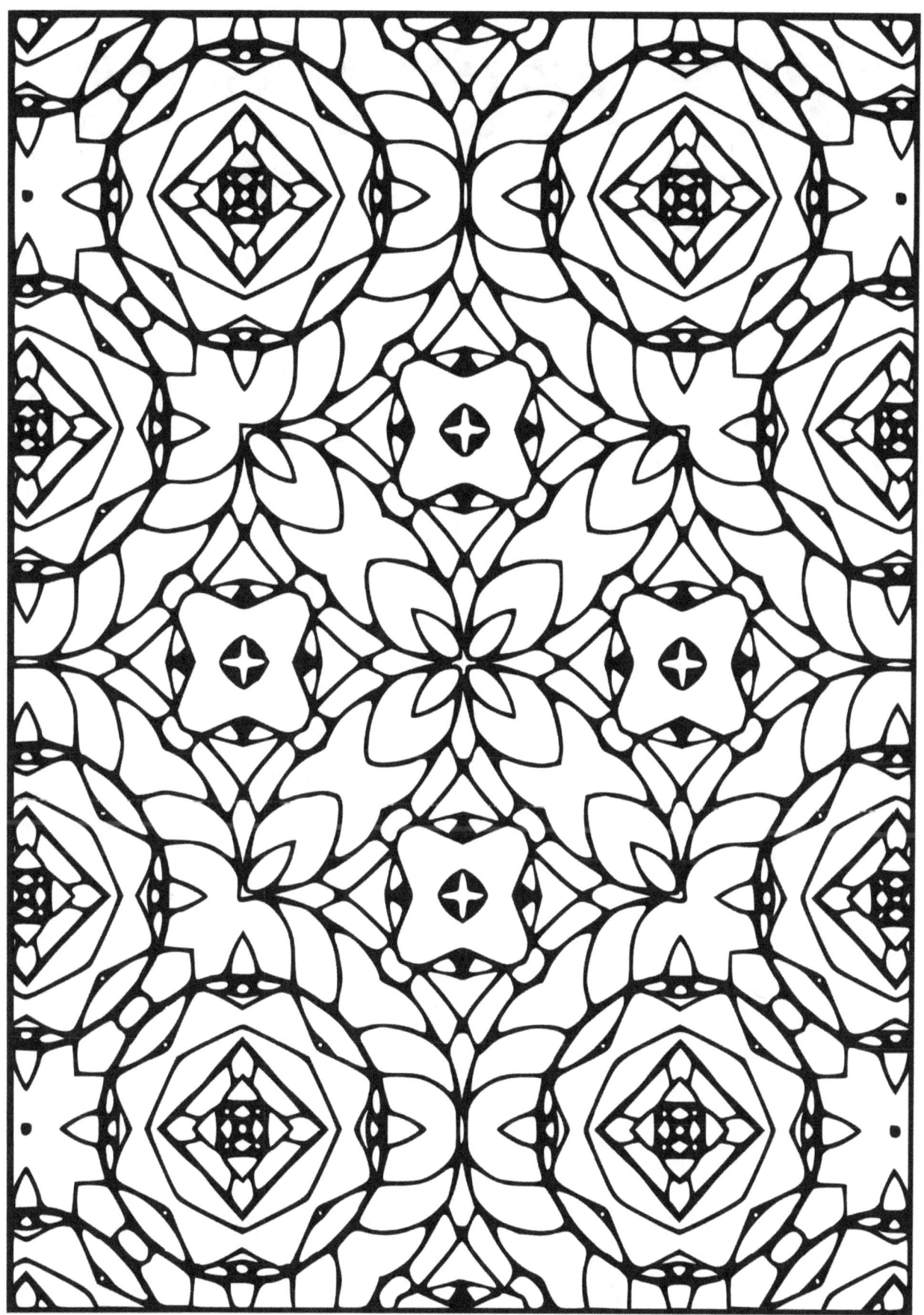

TEST YOUR COLOR

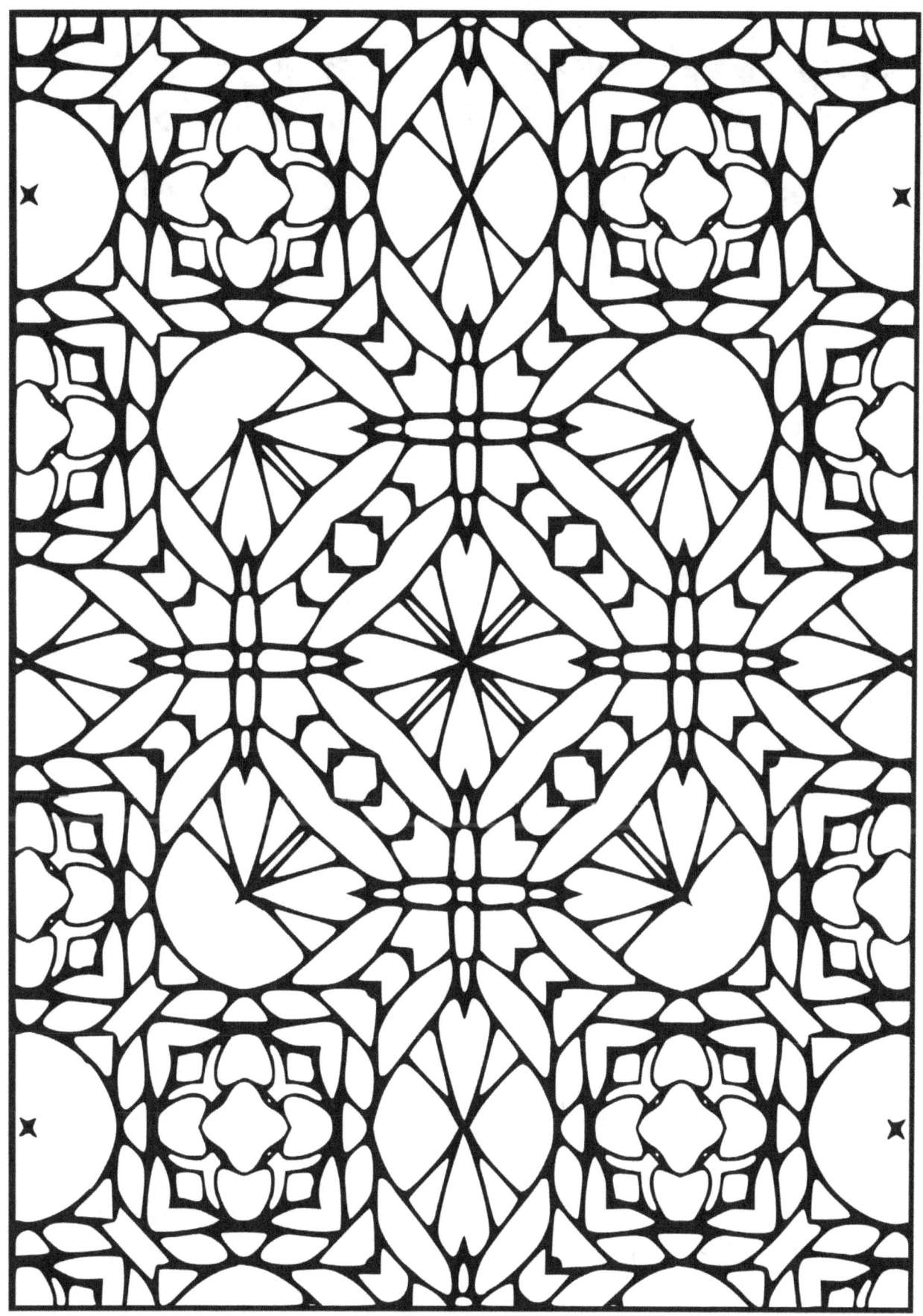

TEST YOUR COLOR

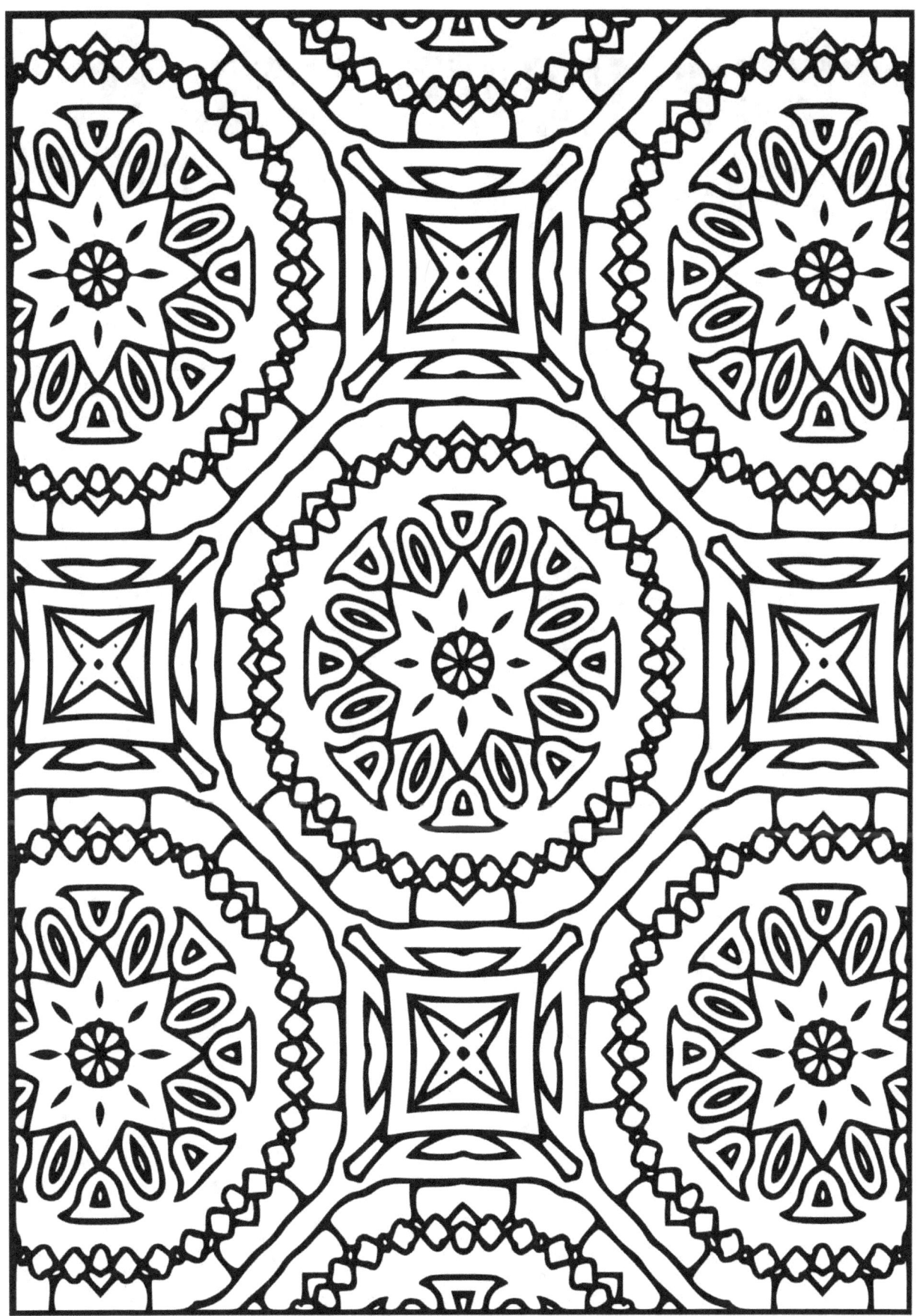

TEST YOUR COLOR

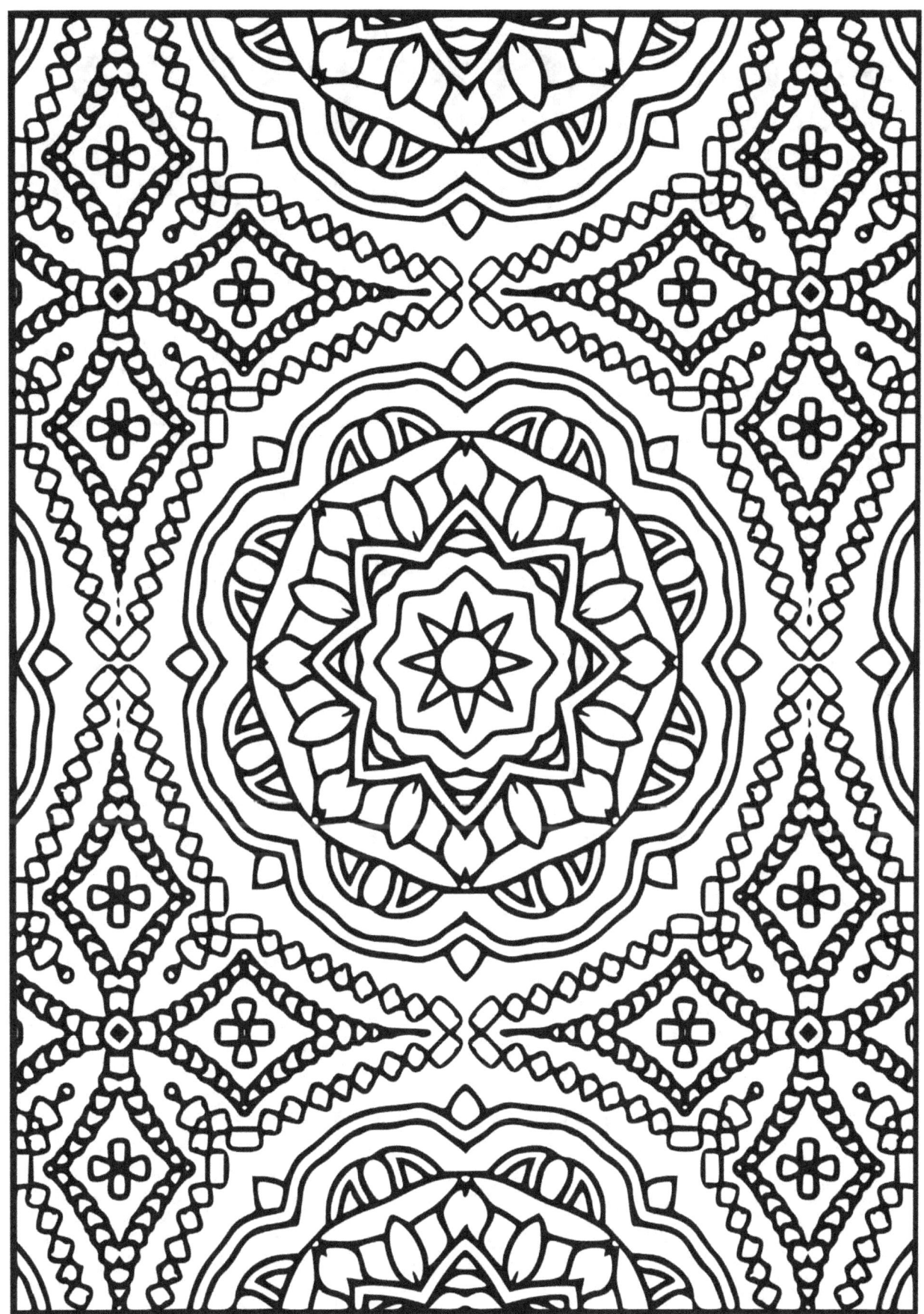

TEST YOUR COLOR

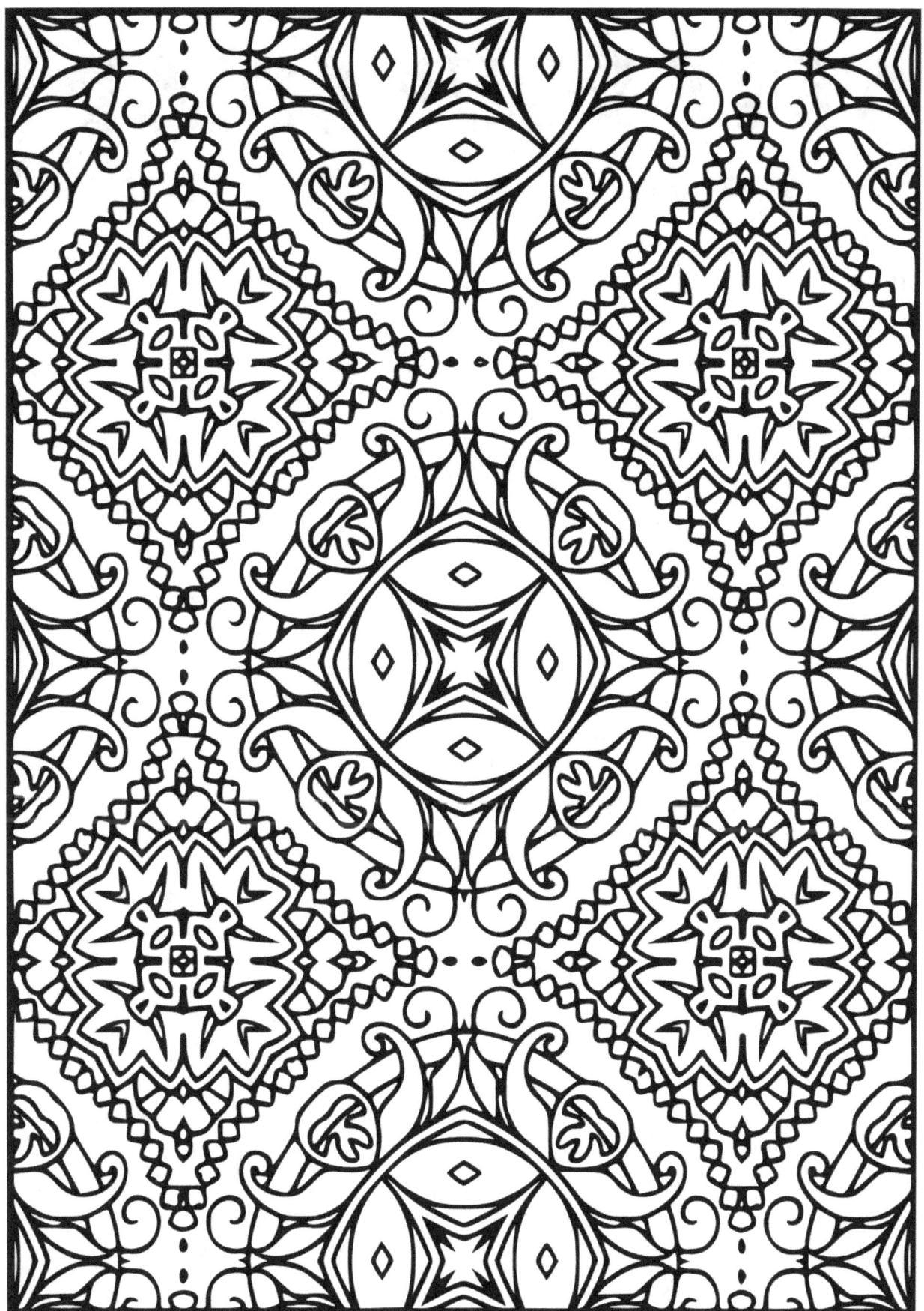

TEST YOUR COLOR

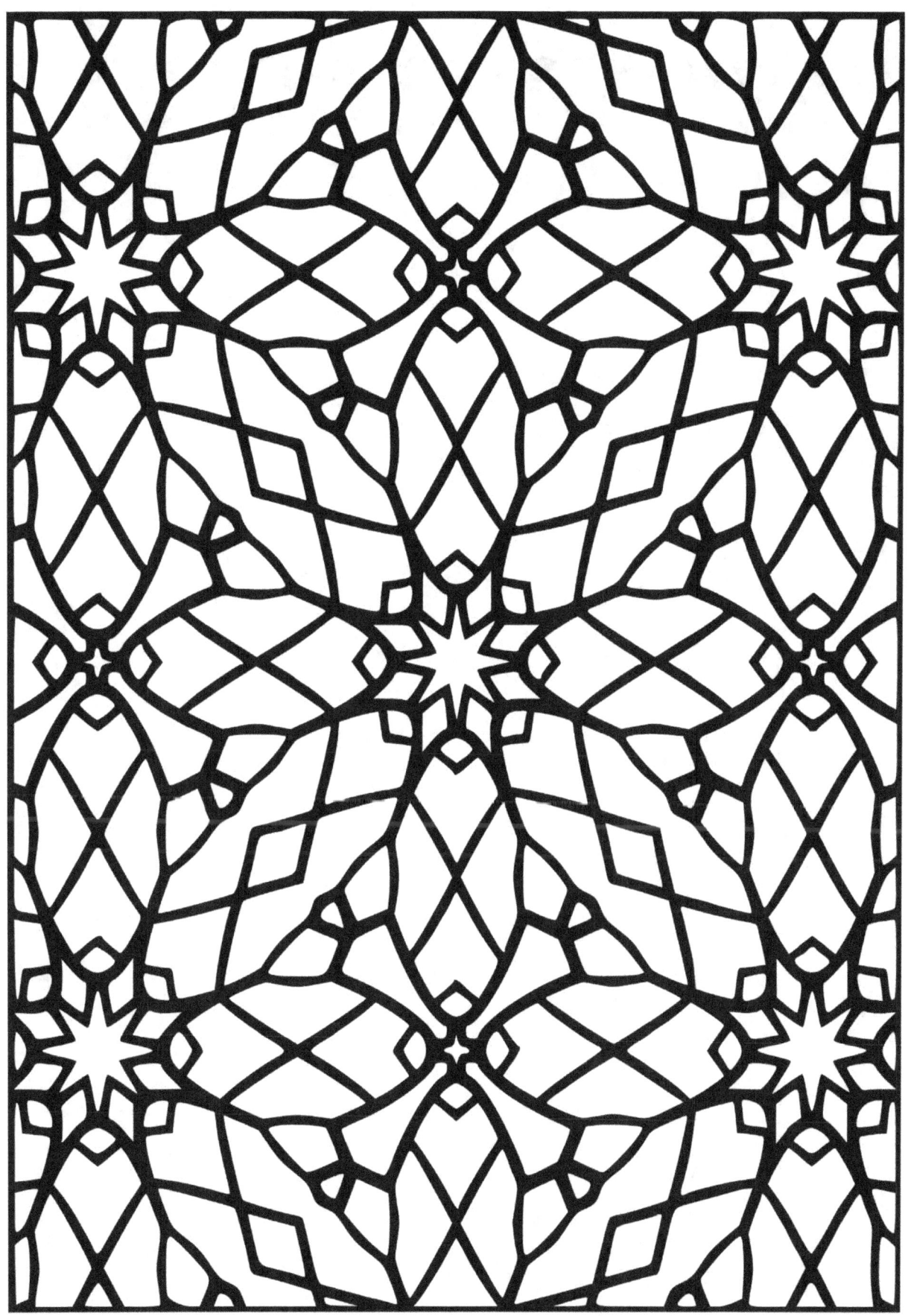

TEST YOUR COLOR

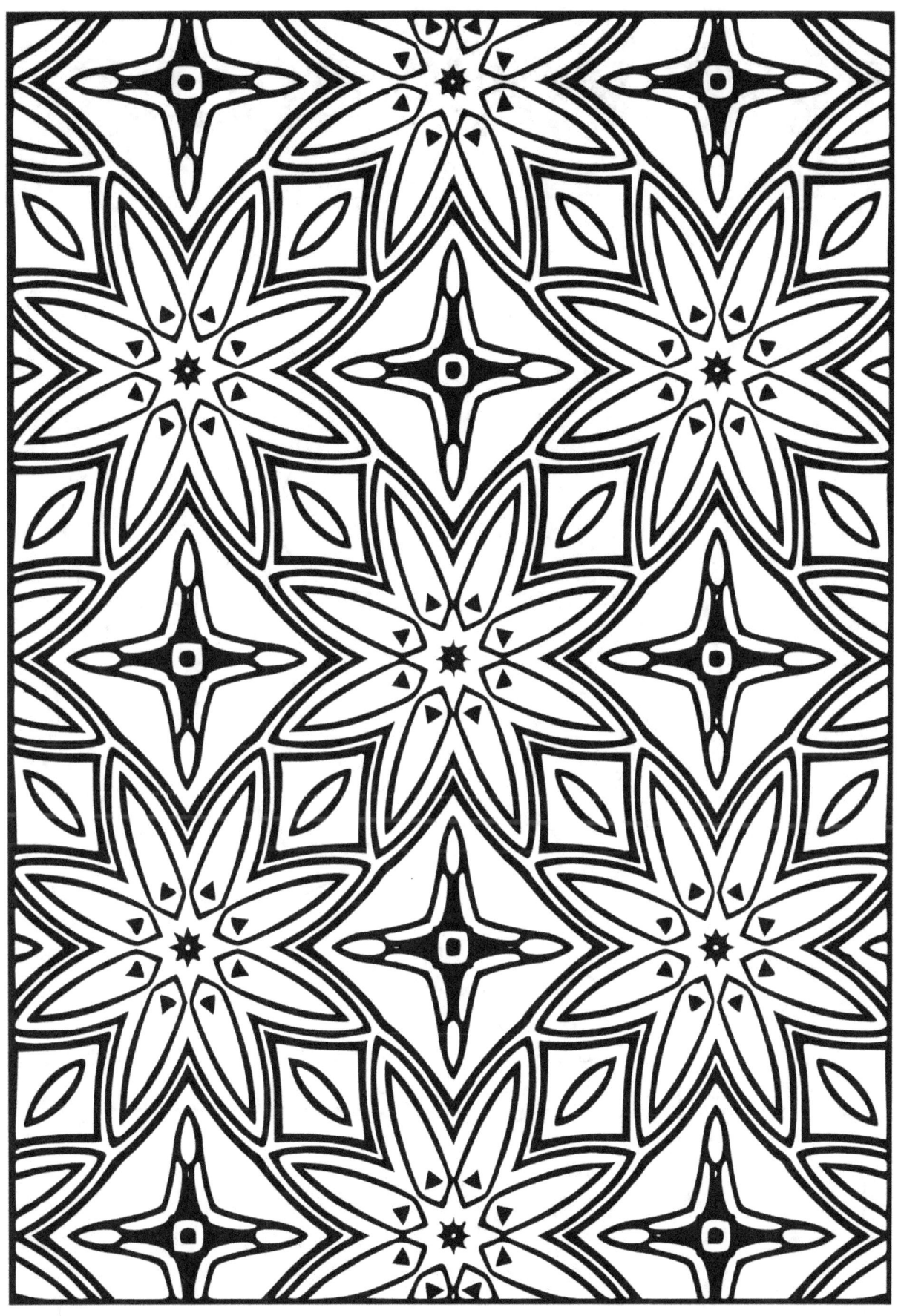

TEST YOUR COLOR

TEST YOUR COLOR

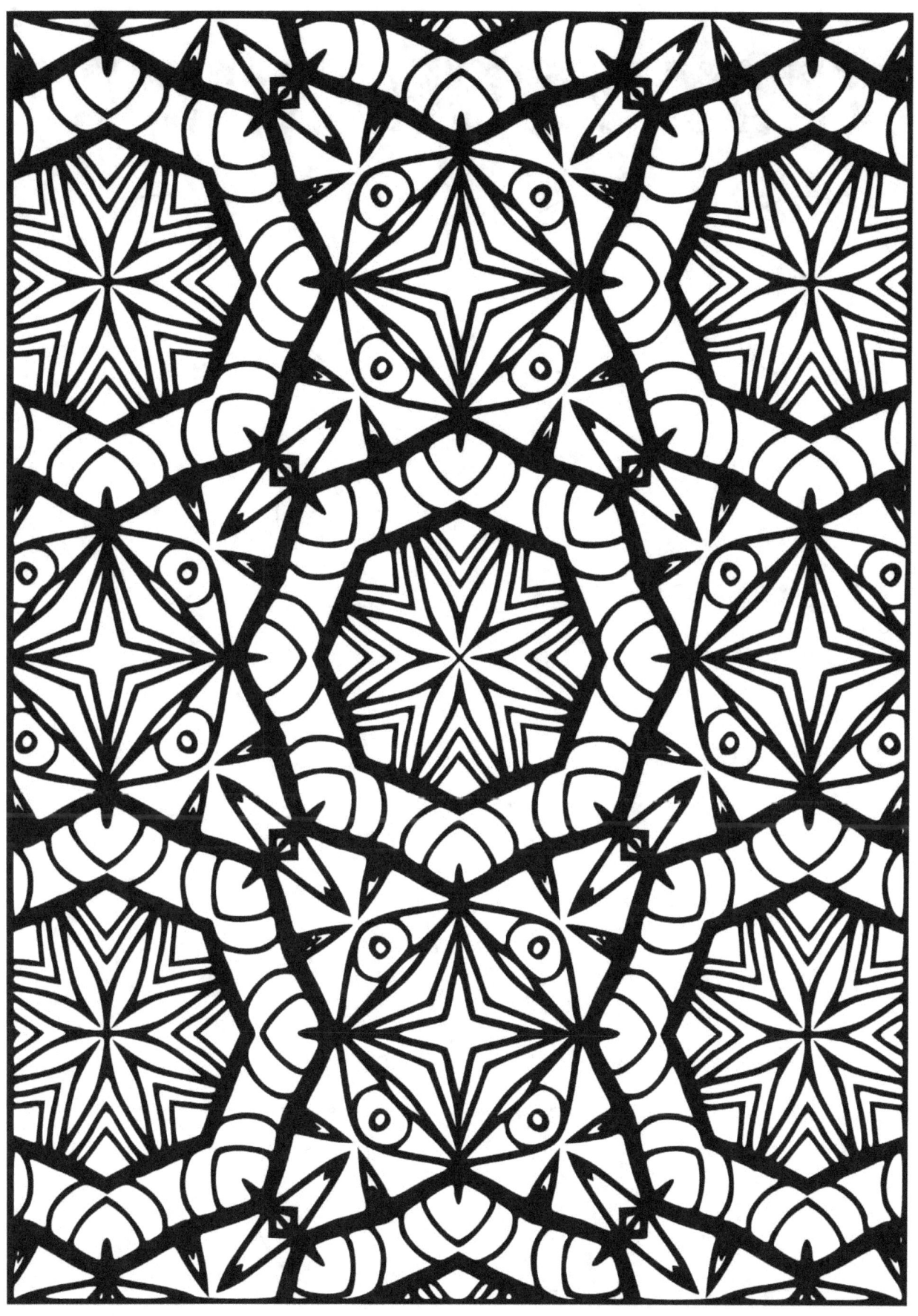

TEST YOUR COLOR

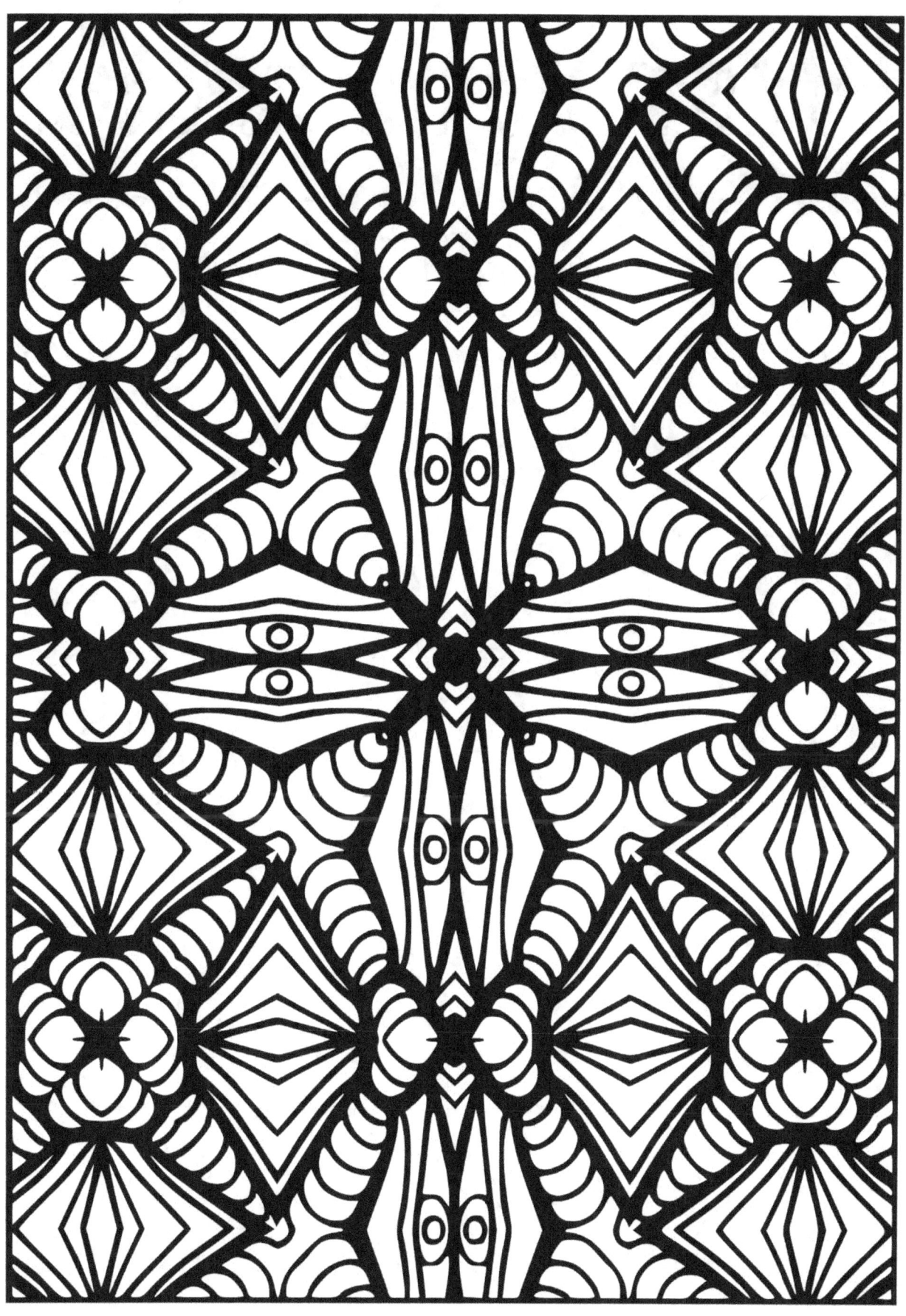

TEST YOUR COLOR

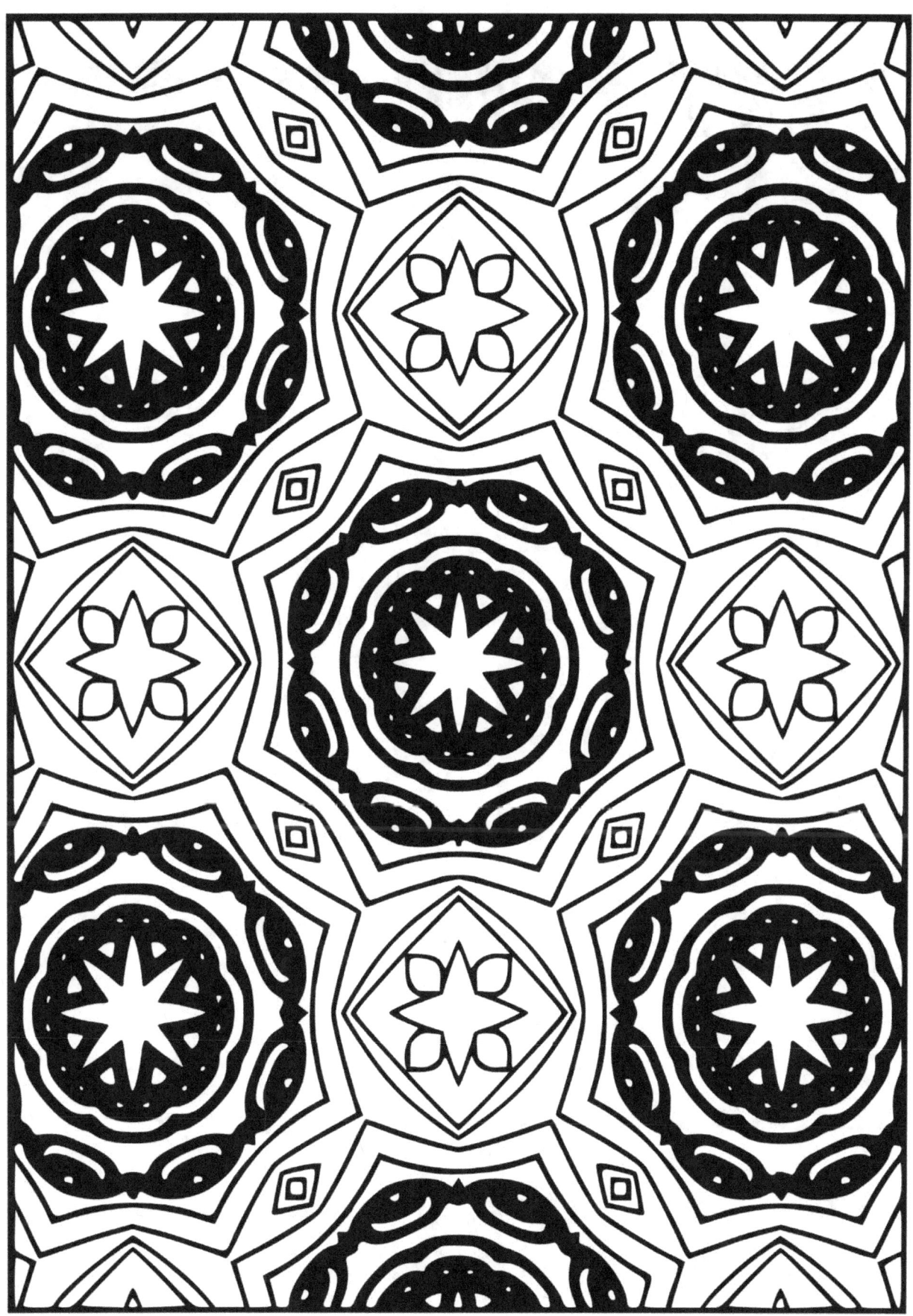

TEST YOUR COLOR

TEST YOUR COLOR

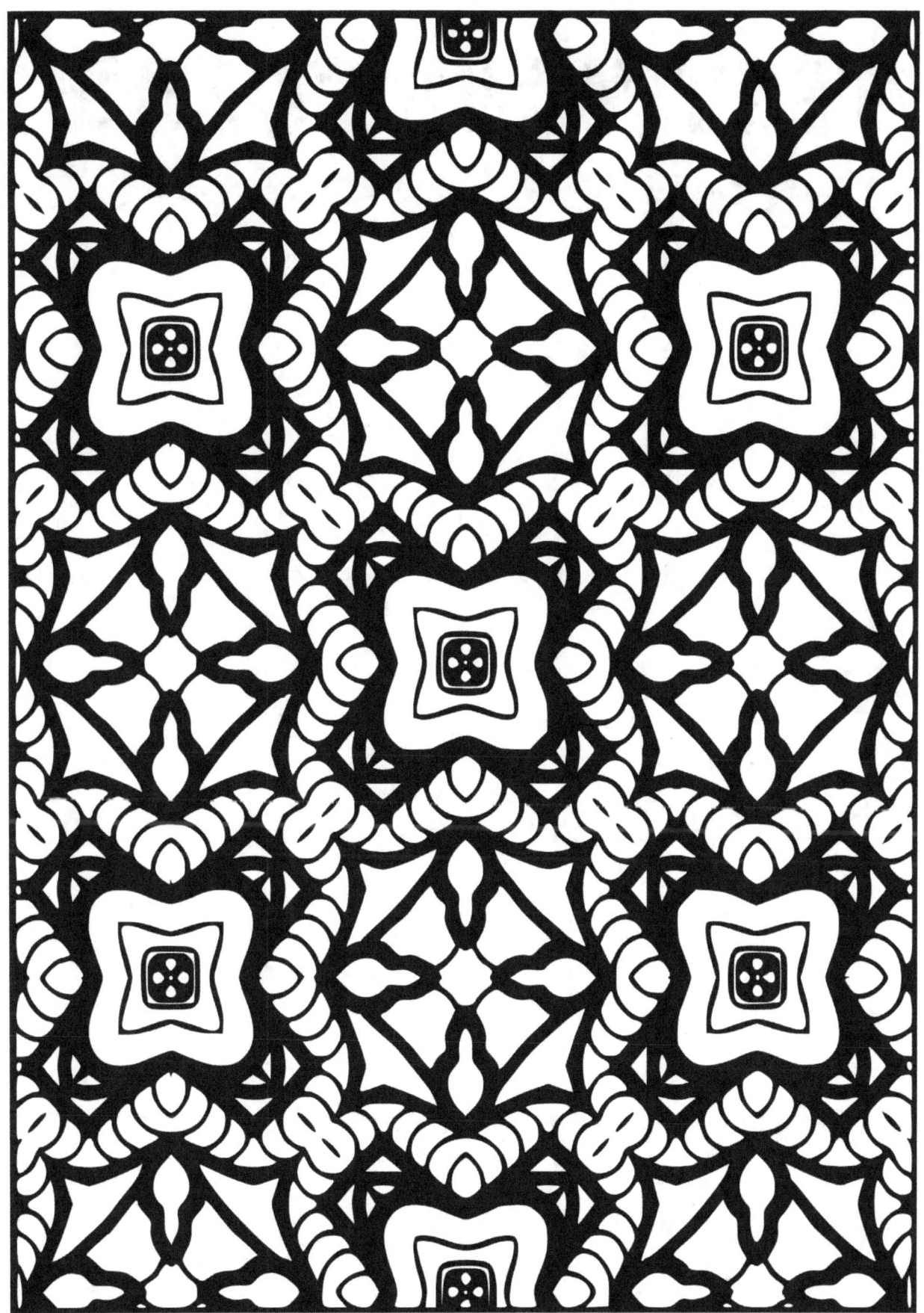

TEST YOUR COLOR

TEST YOUR COLOR

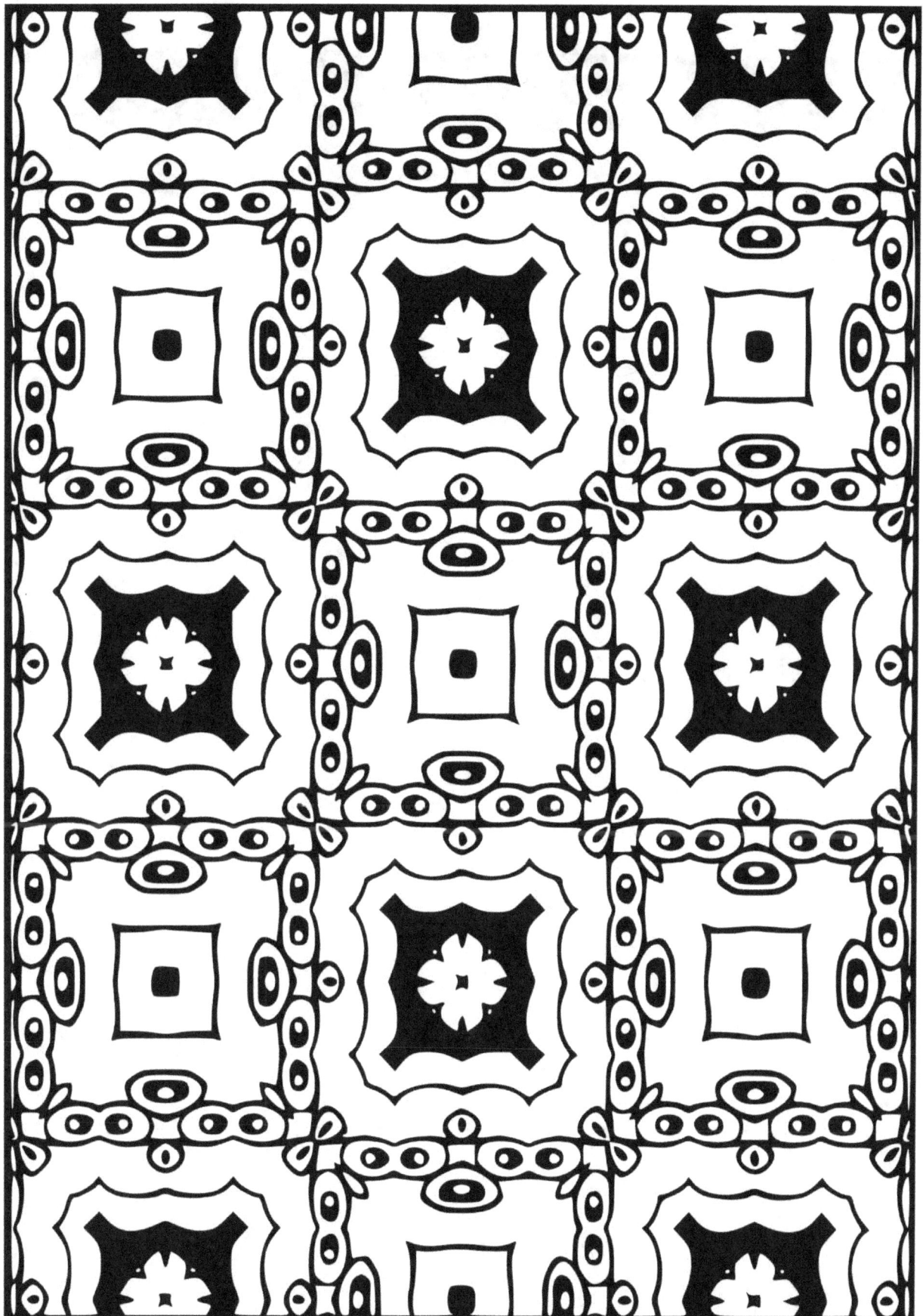

TEST YOUR COLOR

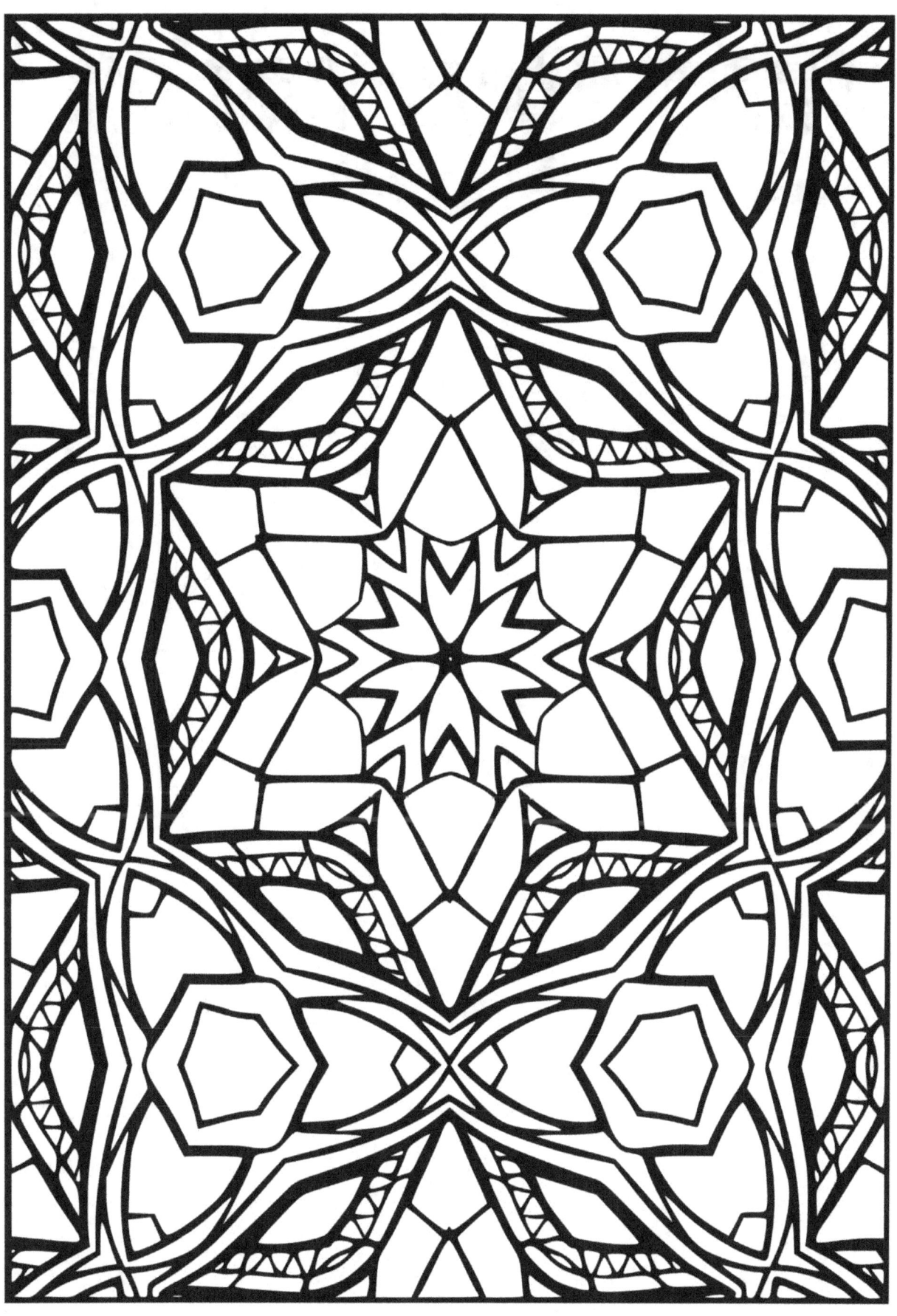

TEST YOUR COLOR

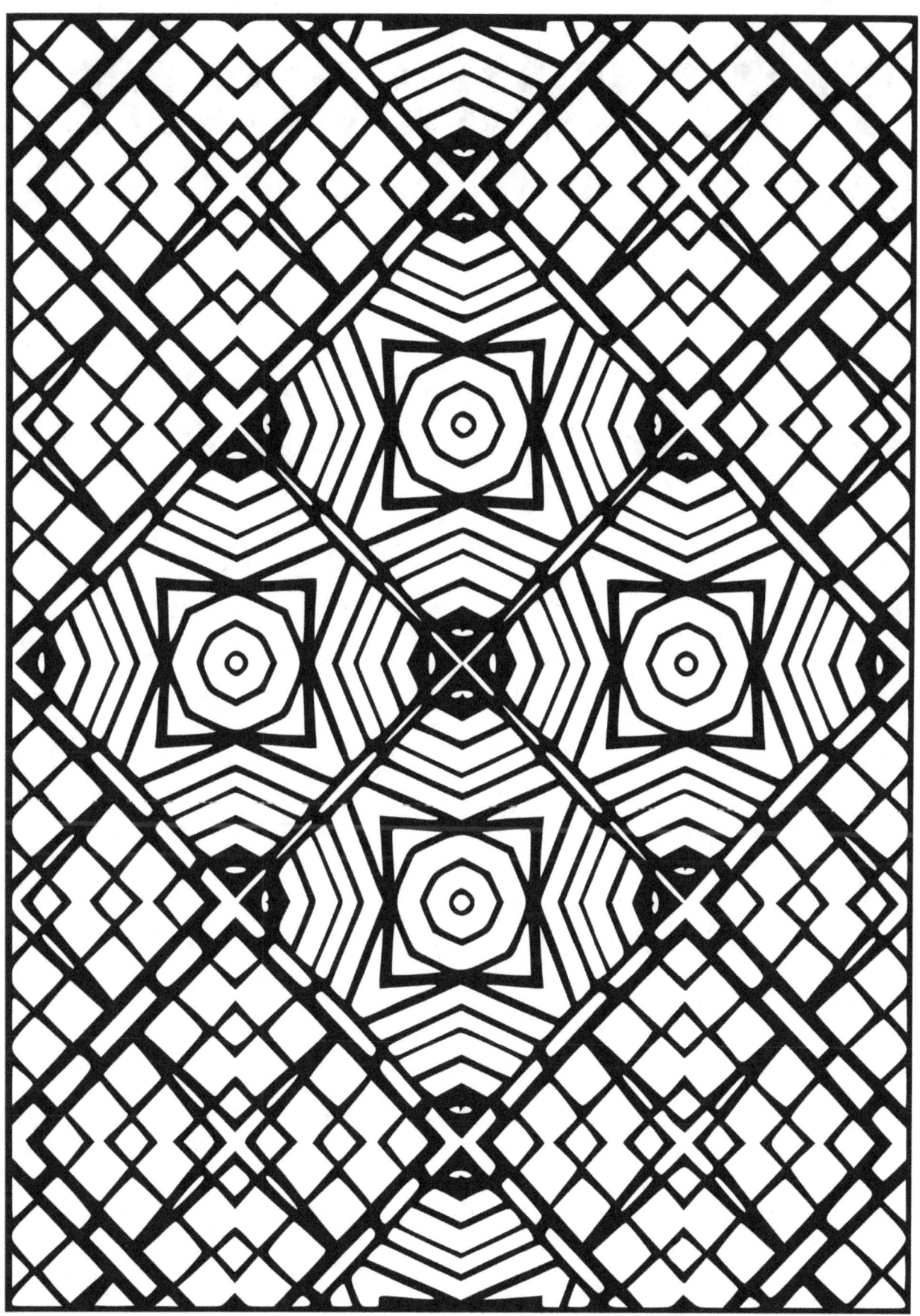

TEST YOUR COLOR

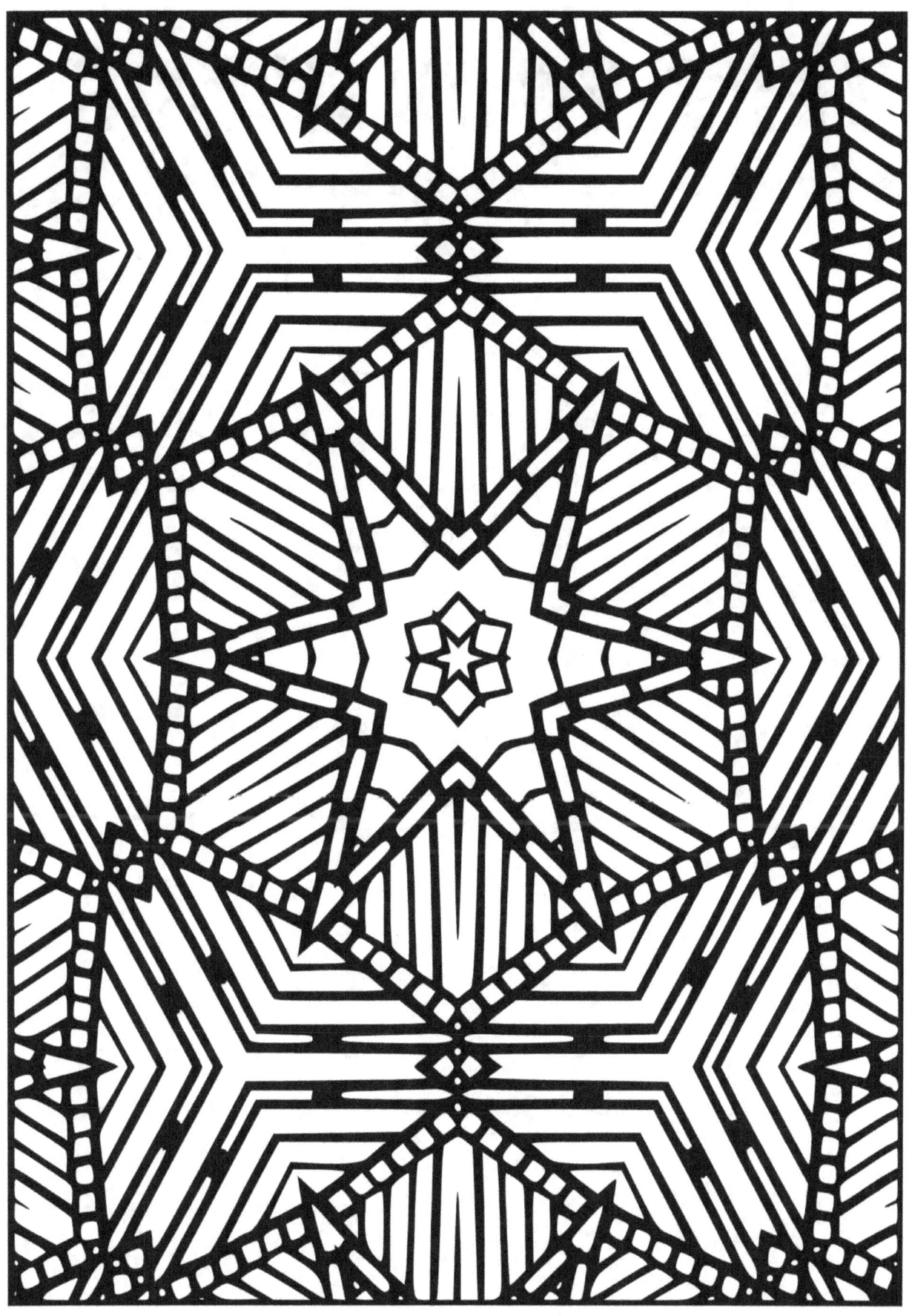

TEST YOUR COLOR

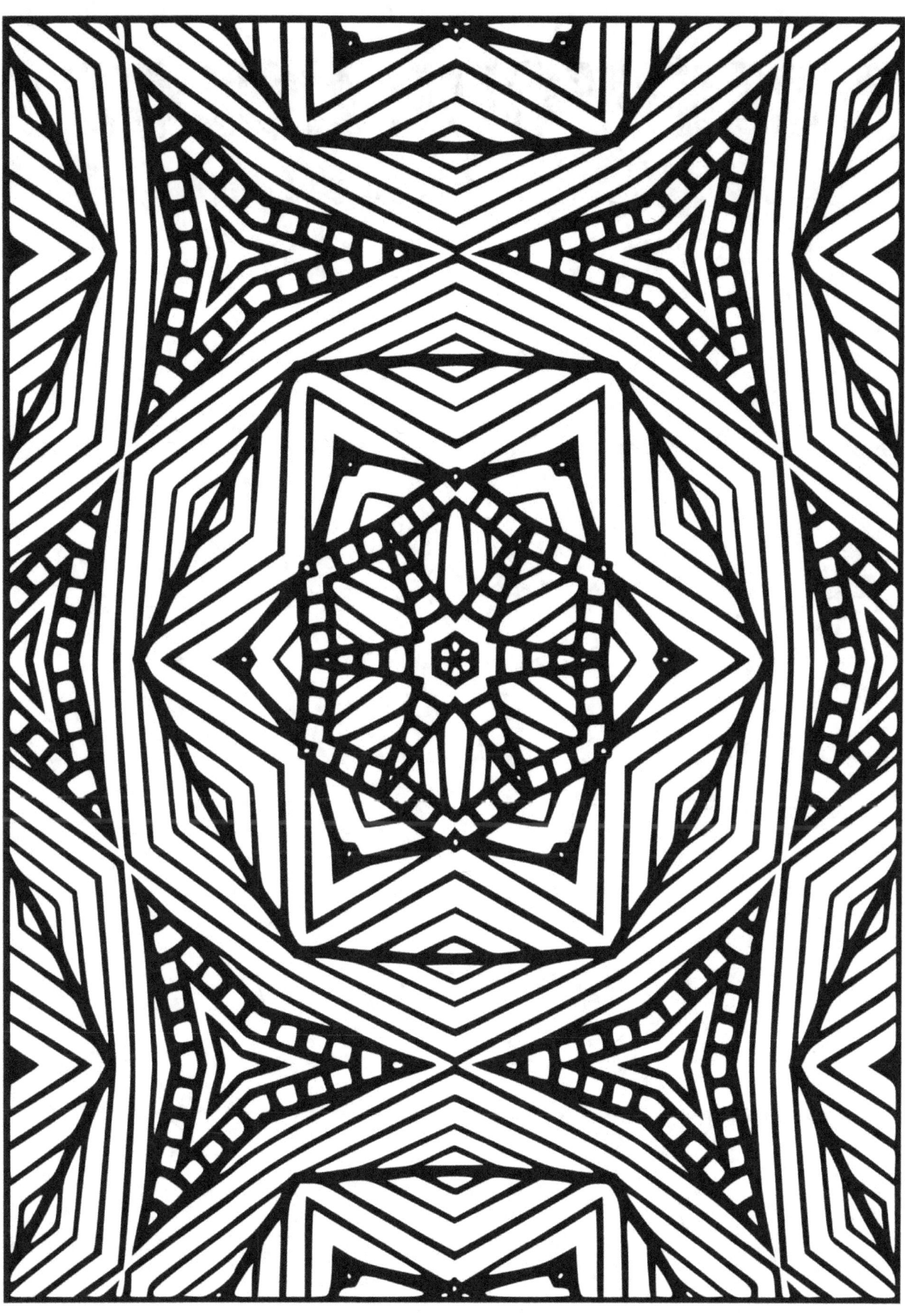

TEST YOUR COLOR

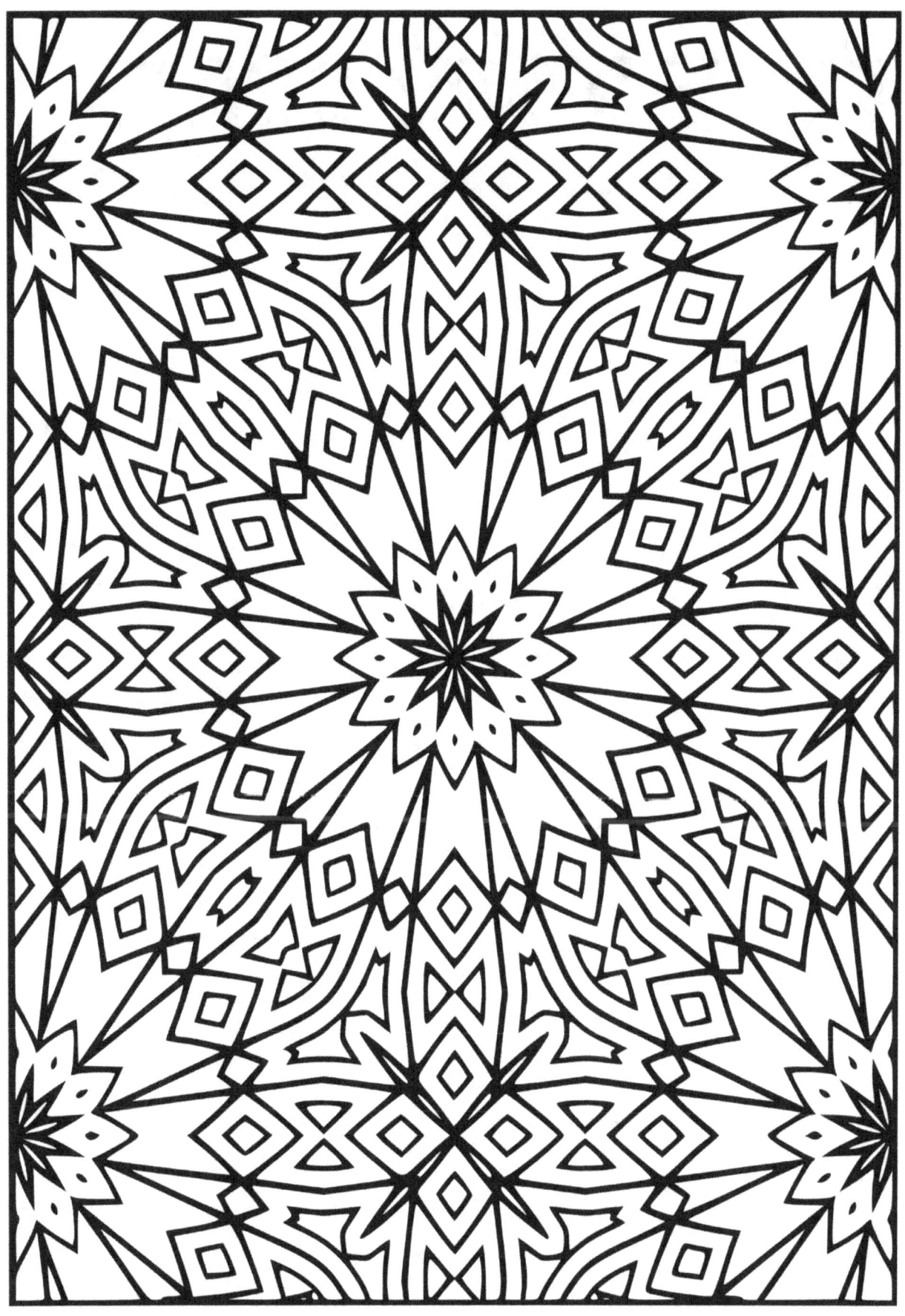

TEST YOUR COLOR

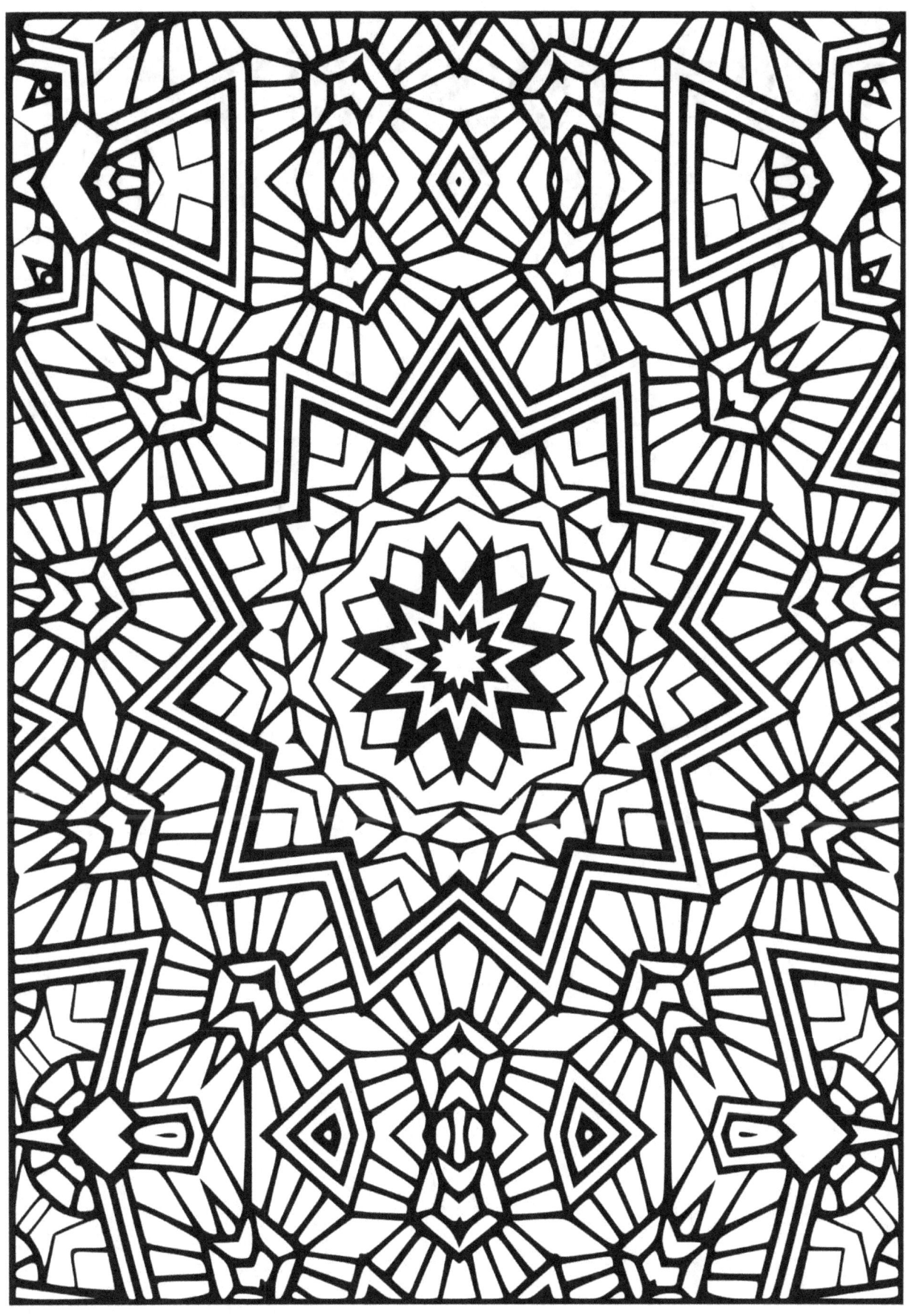

TEST YOUR COLOR

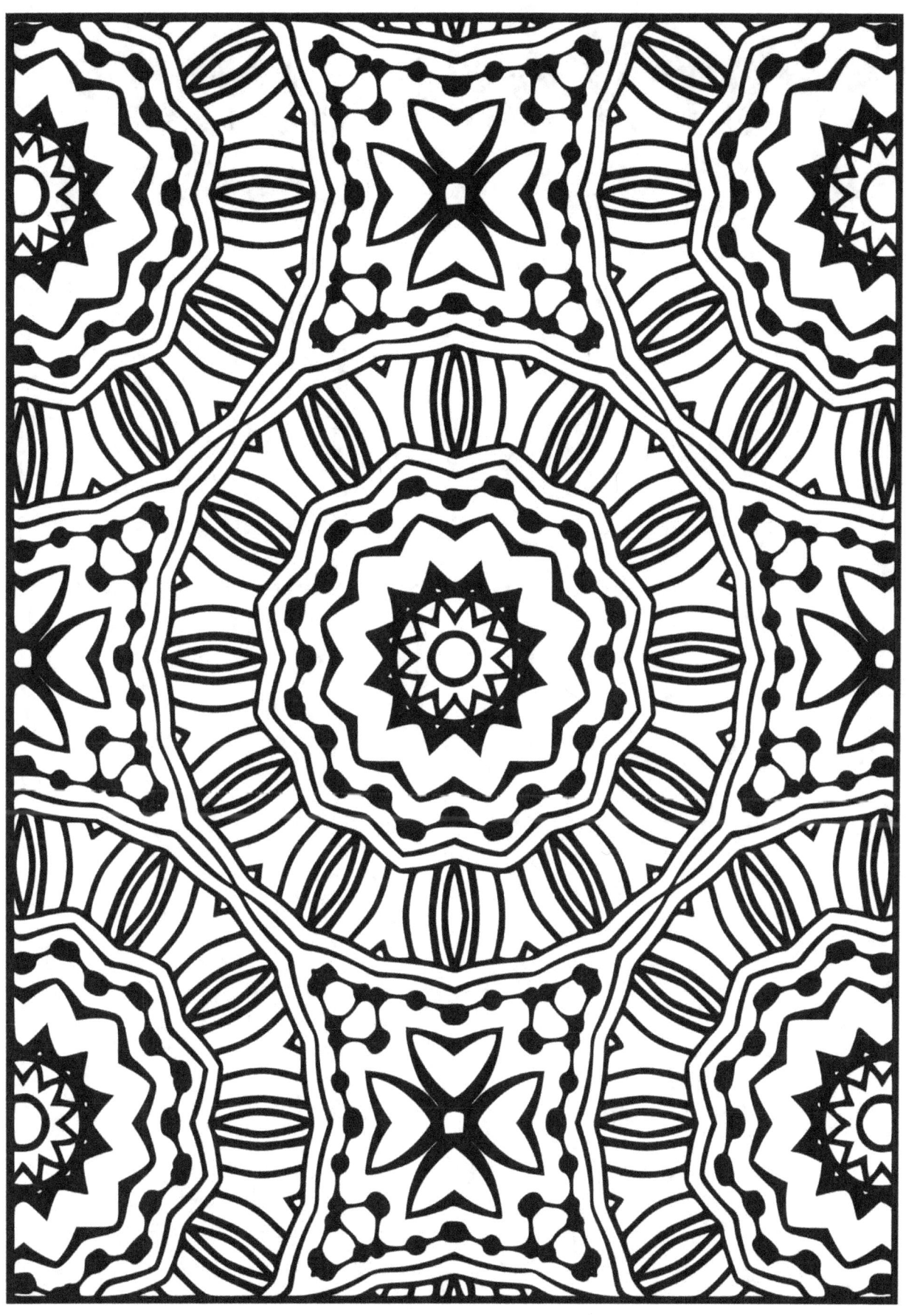

TEST YOUR COLOR

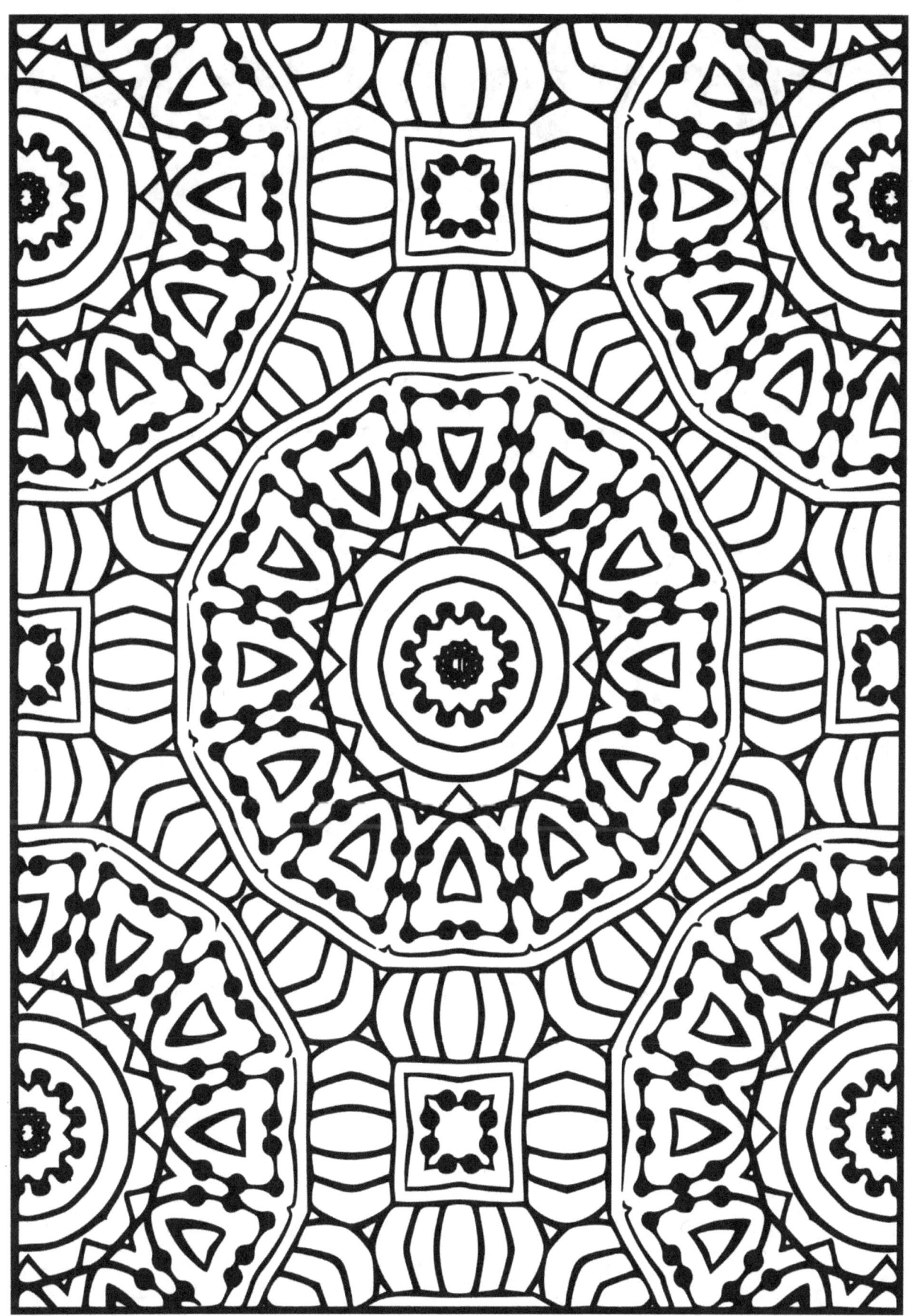

TEST YOUR COLOR

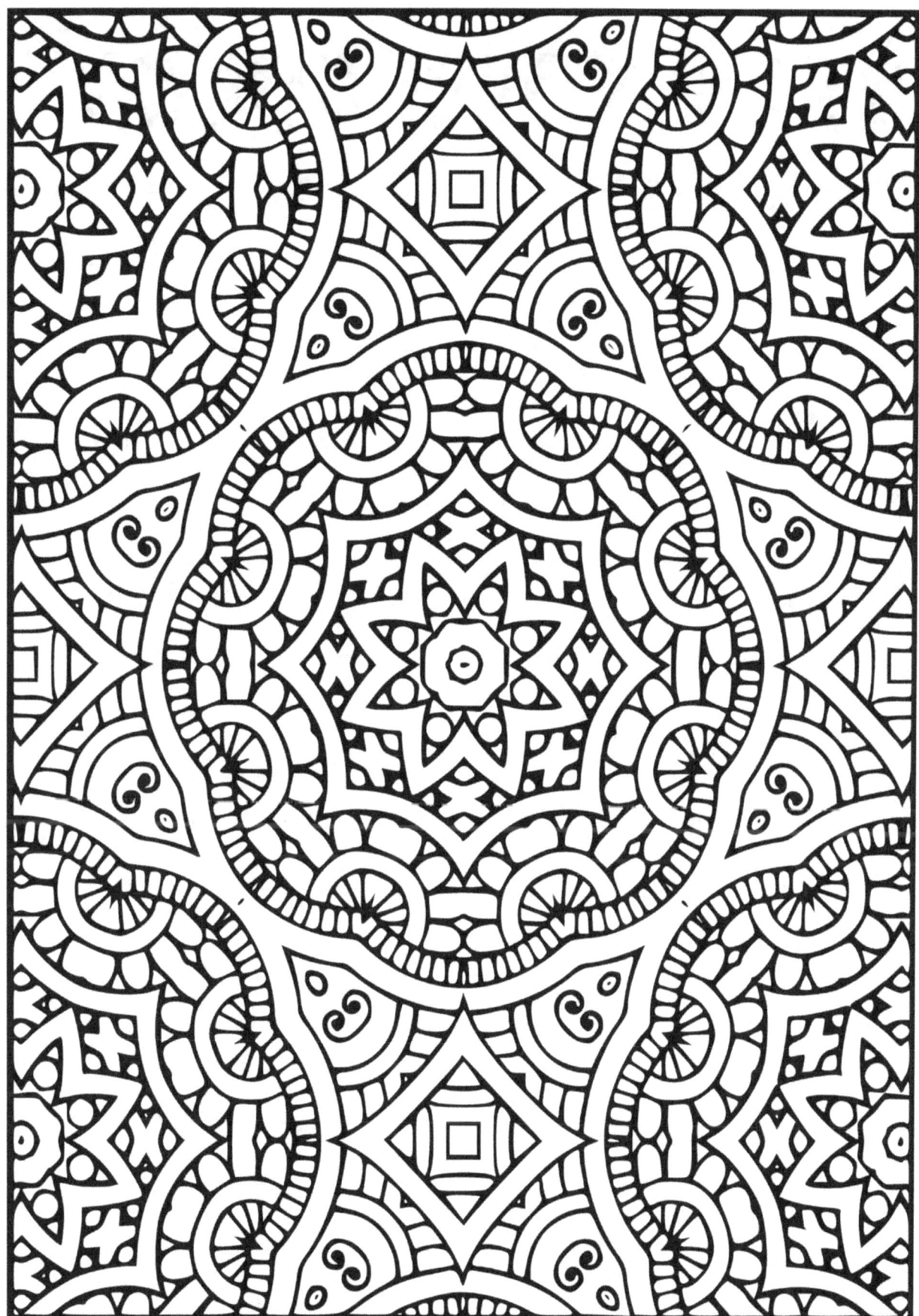

TEST YOUR COLOR

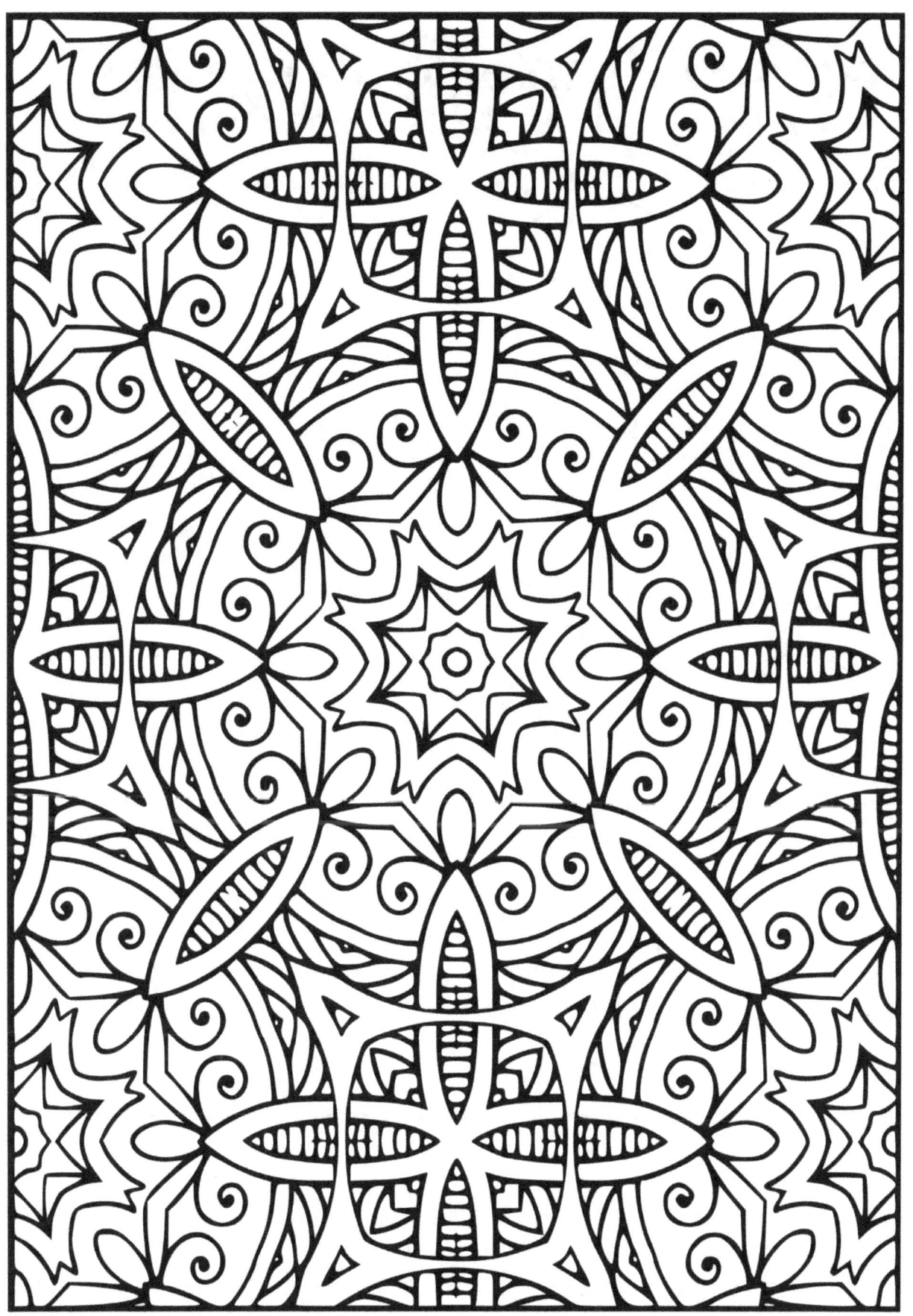

TEST YOUR COLOR

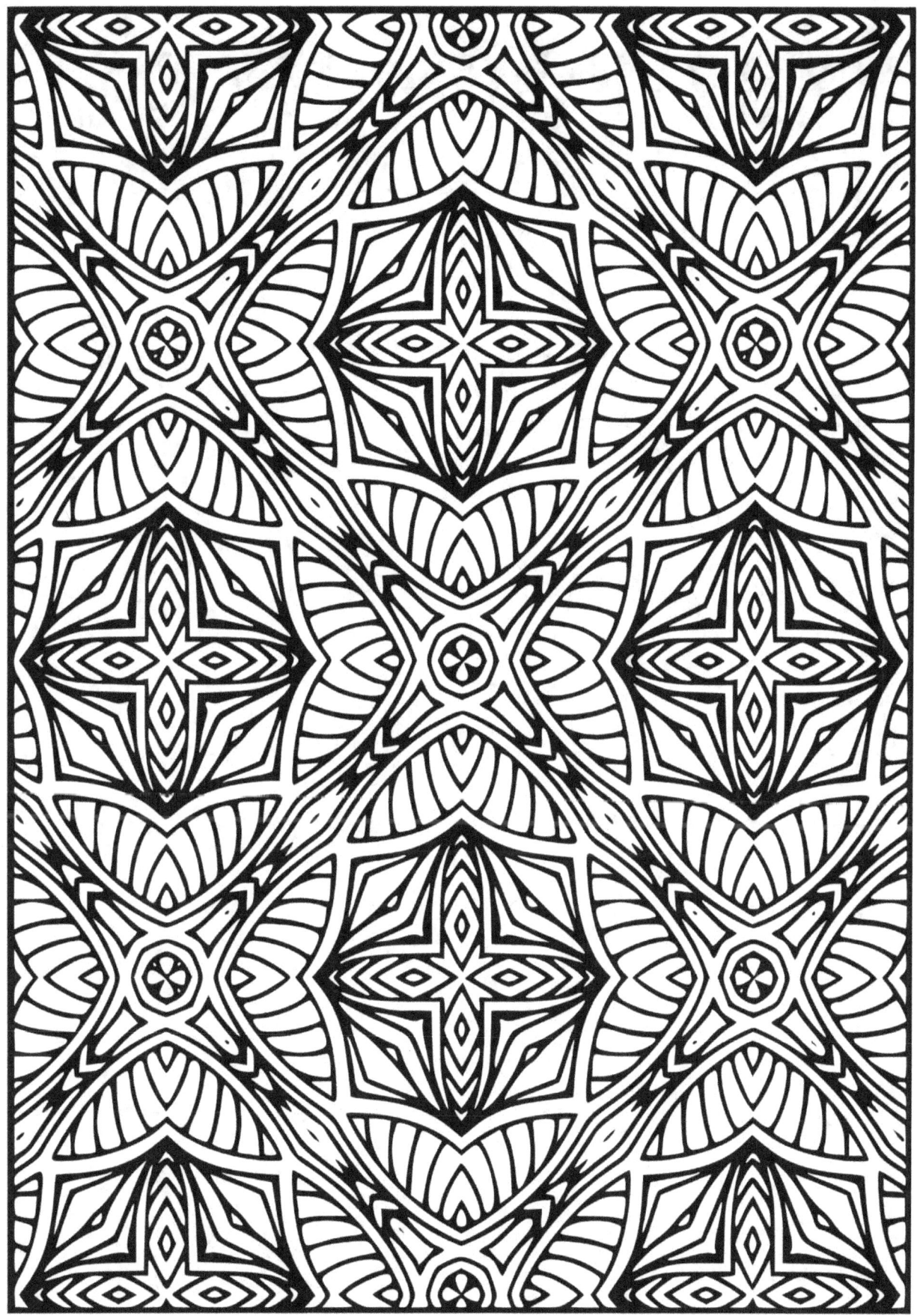

TEST YOUR COLOR

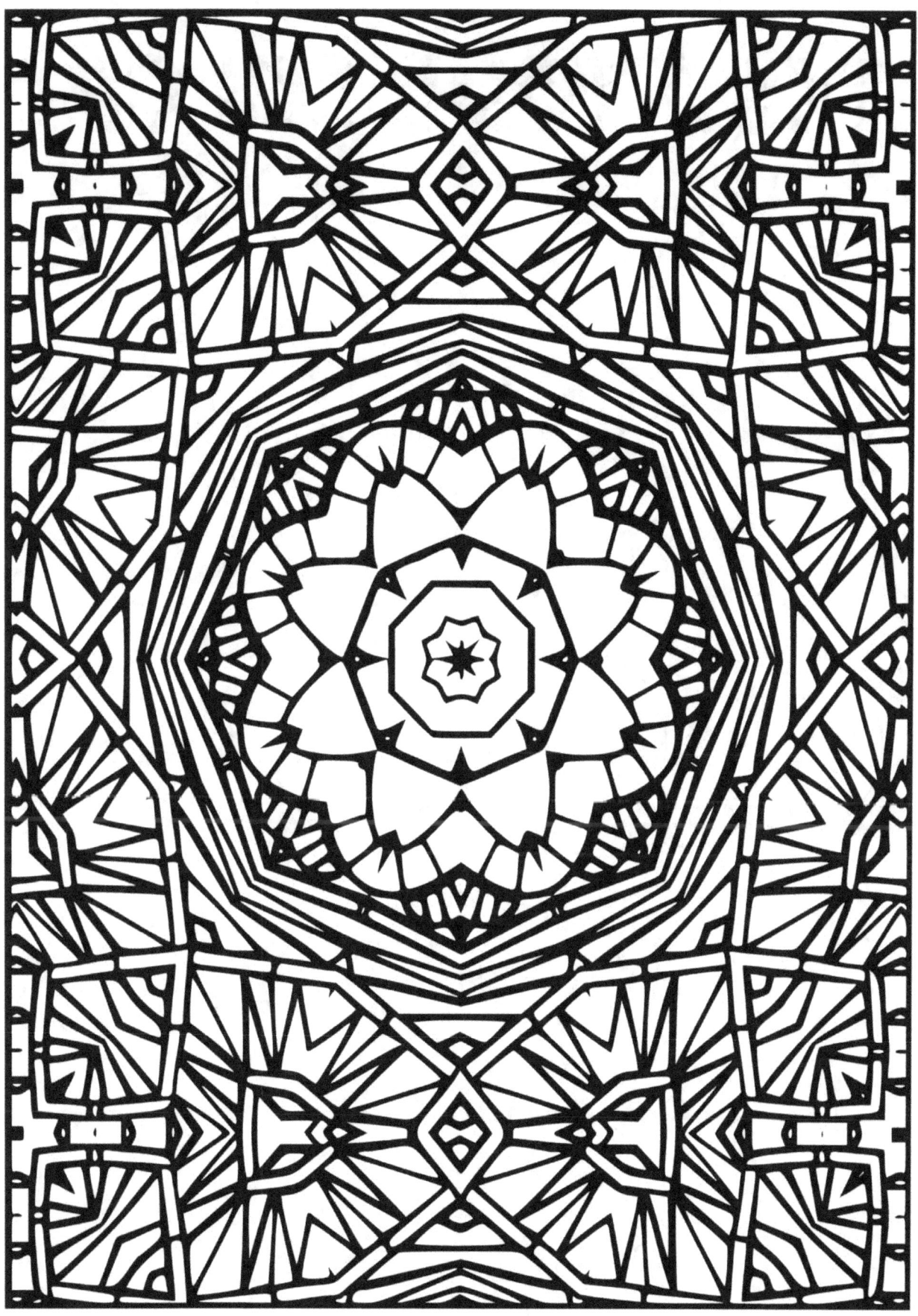

TEST YOUR COLOR

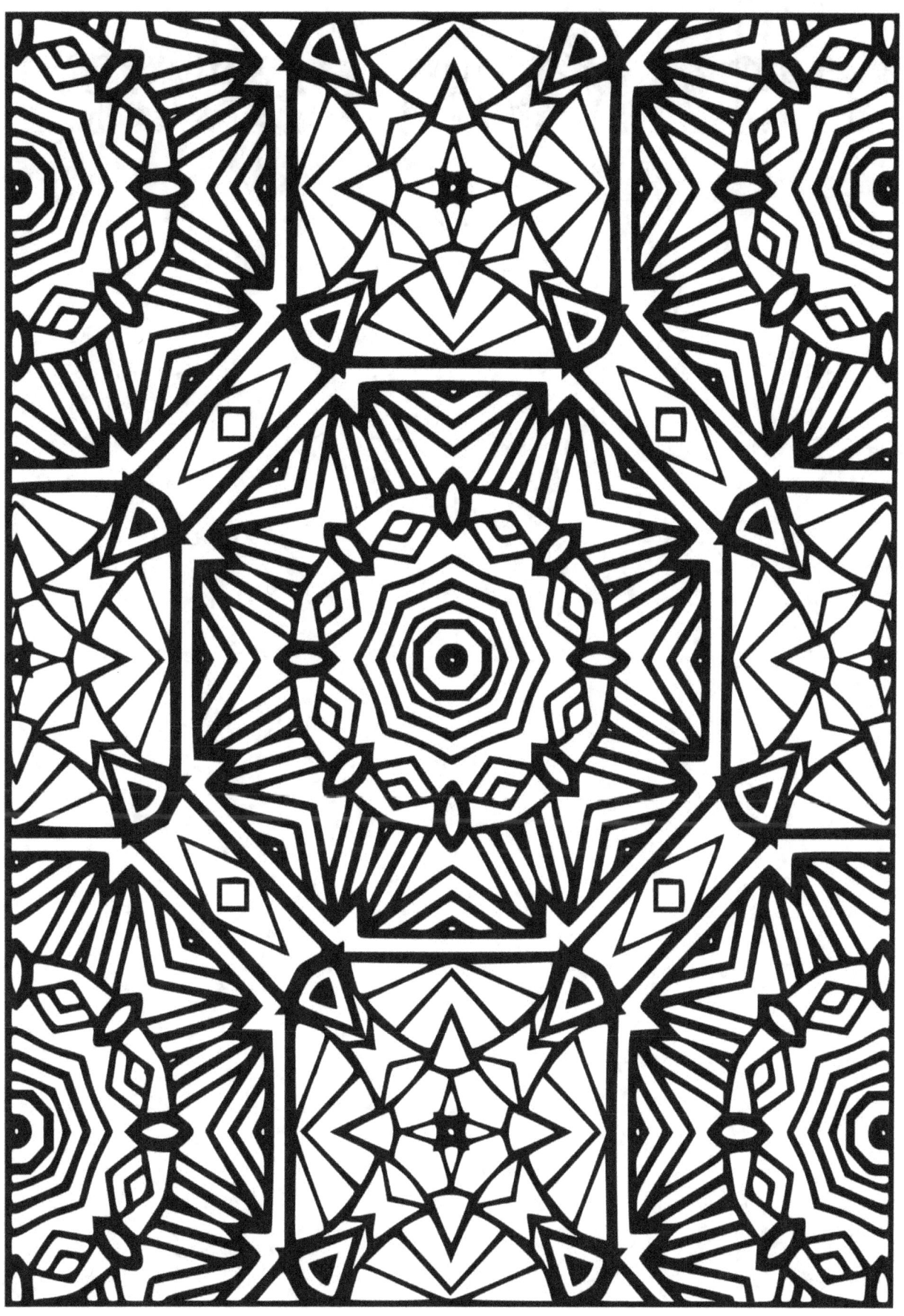

TEST YOUR COLOR

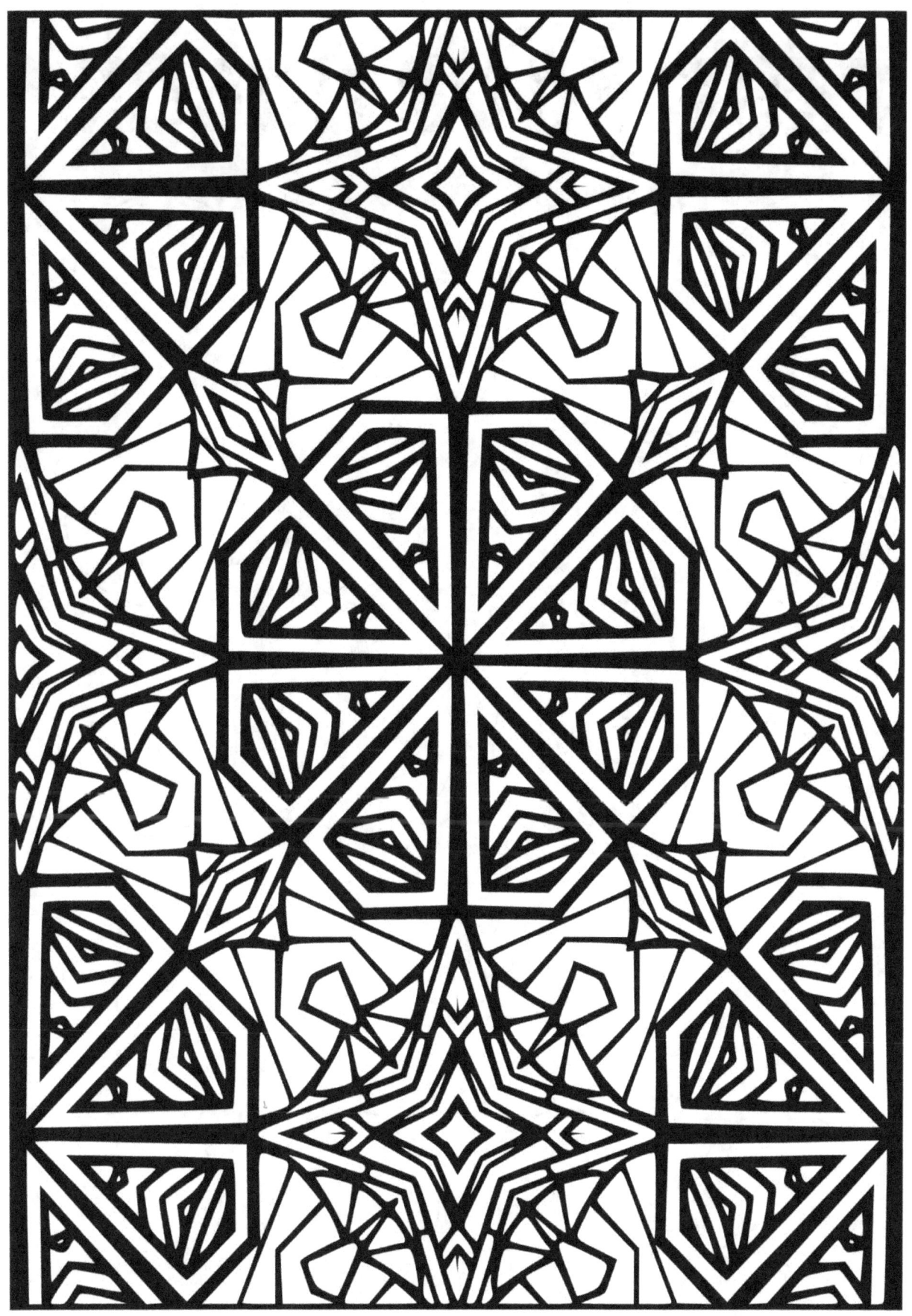

TEST YOUR COLOR

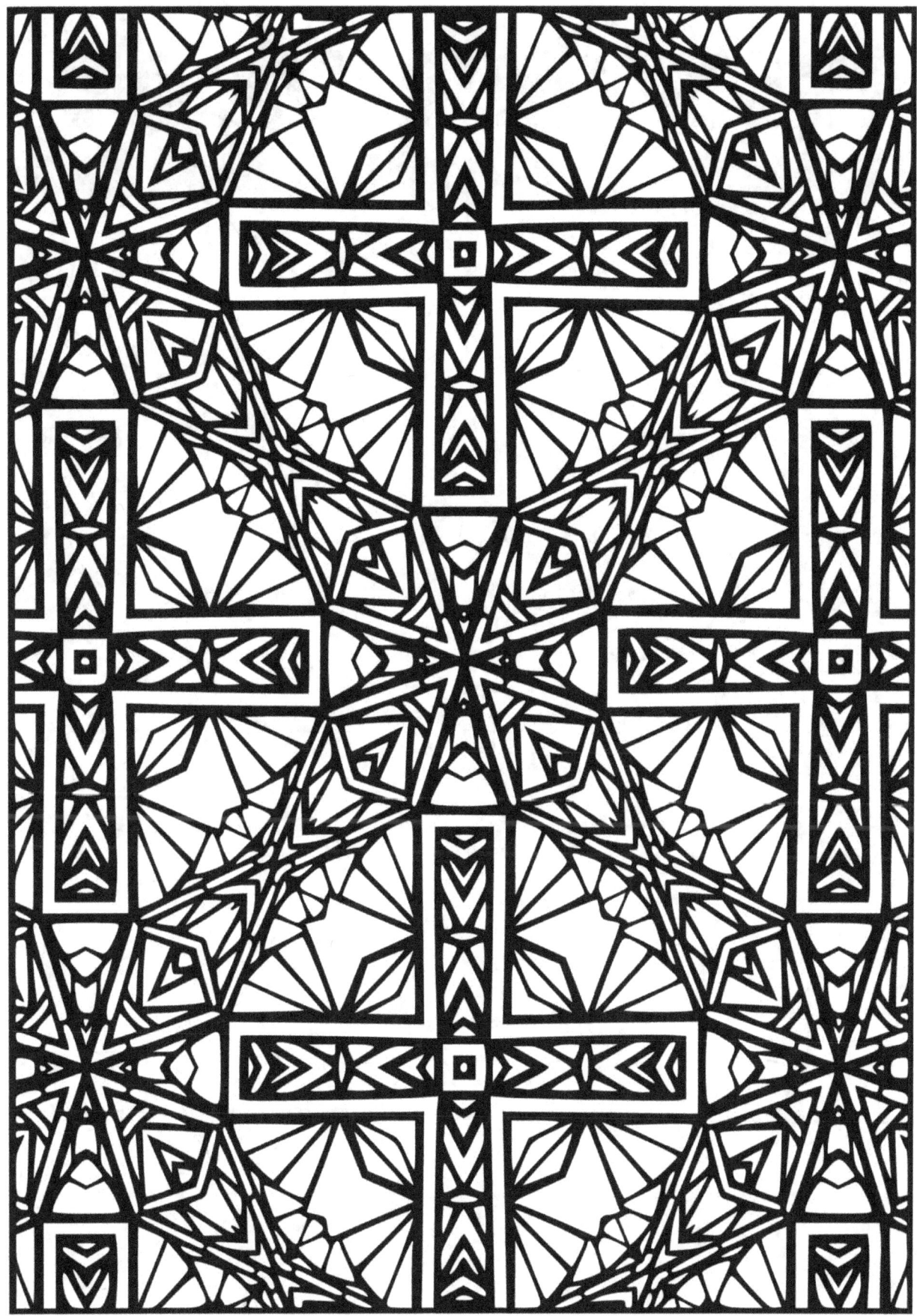

TEST YOUR COLOR

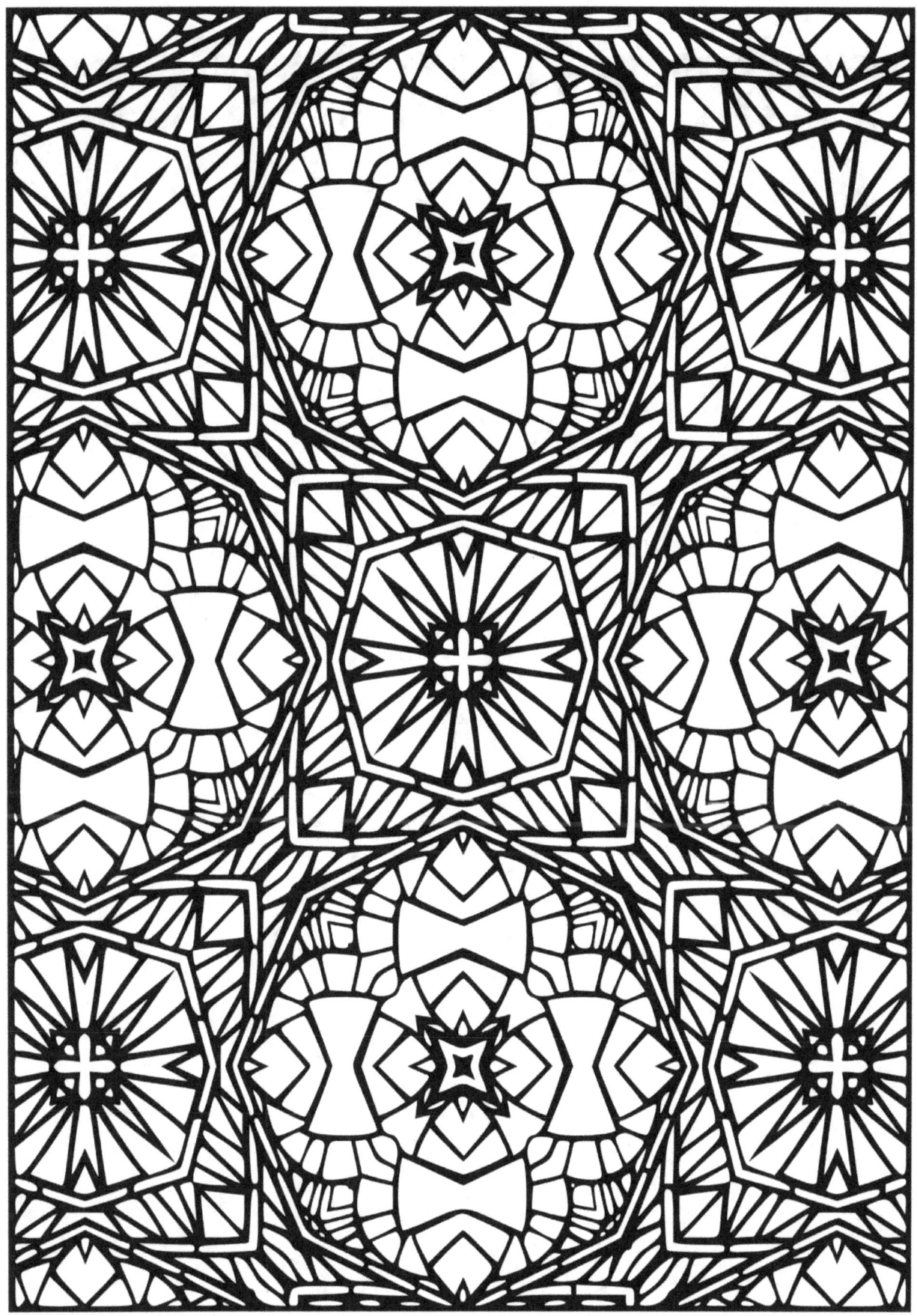

TEST YOUR COLOR

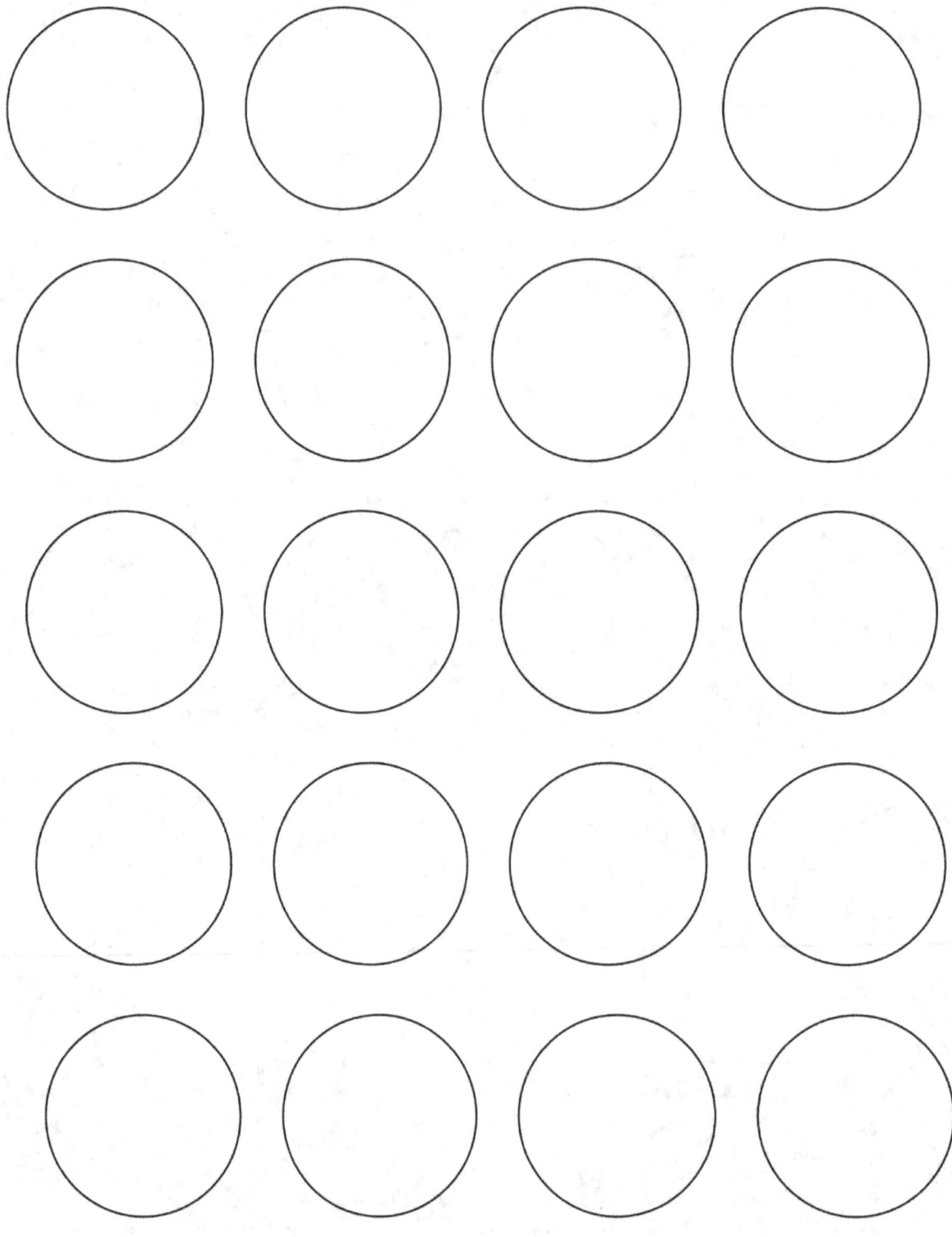

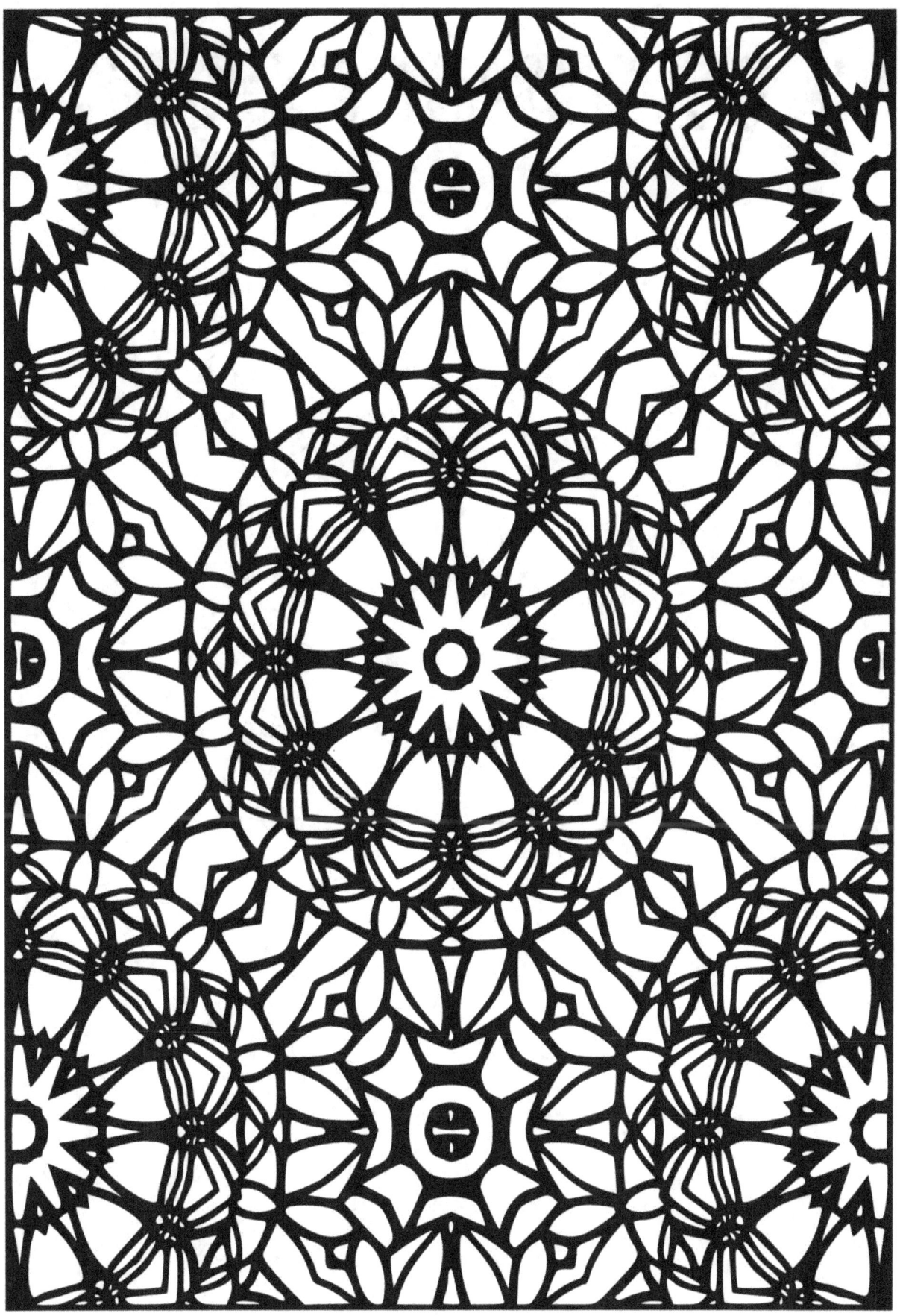

TEST YOUR COLOR

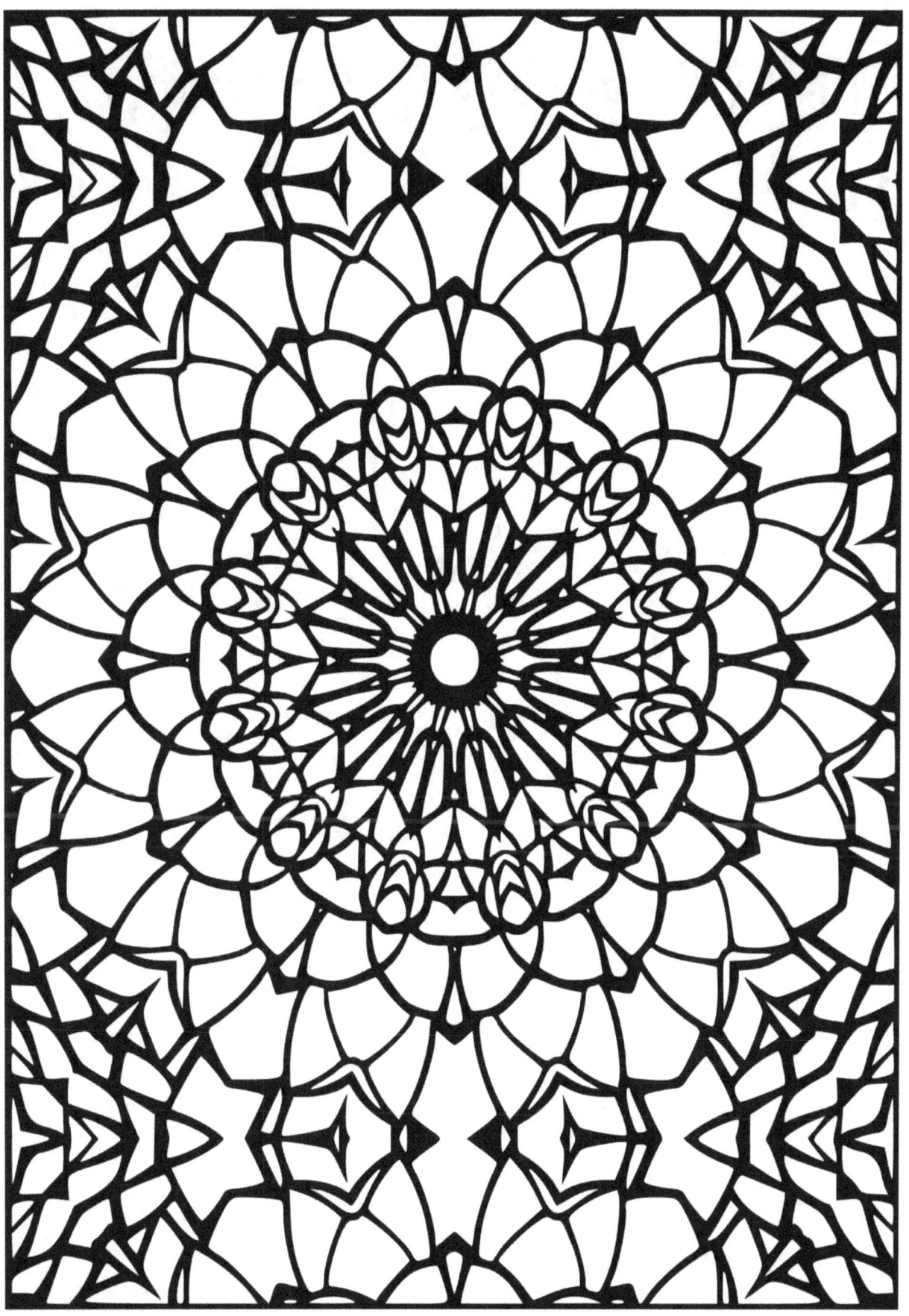

TEST YOUR COLOR

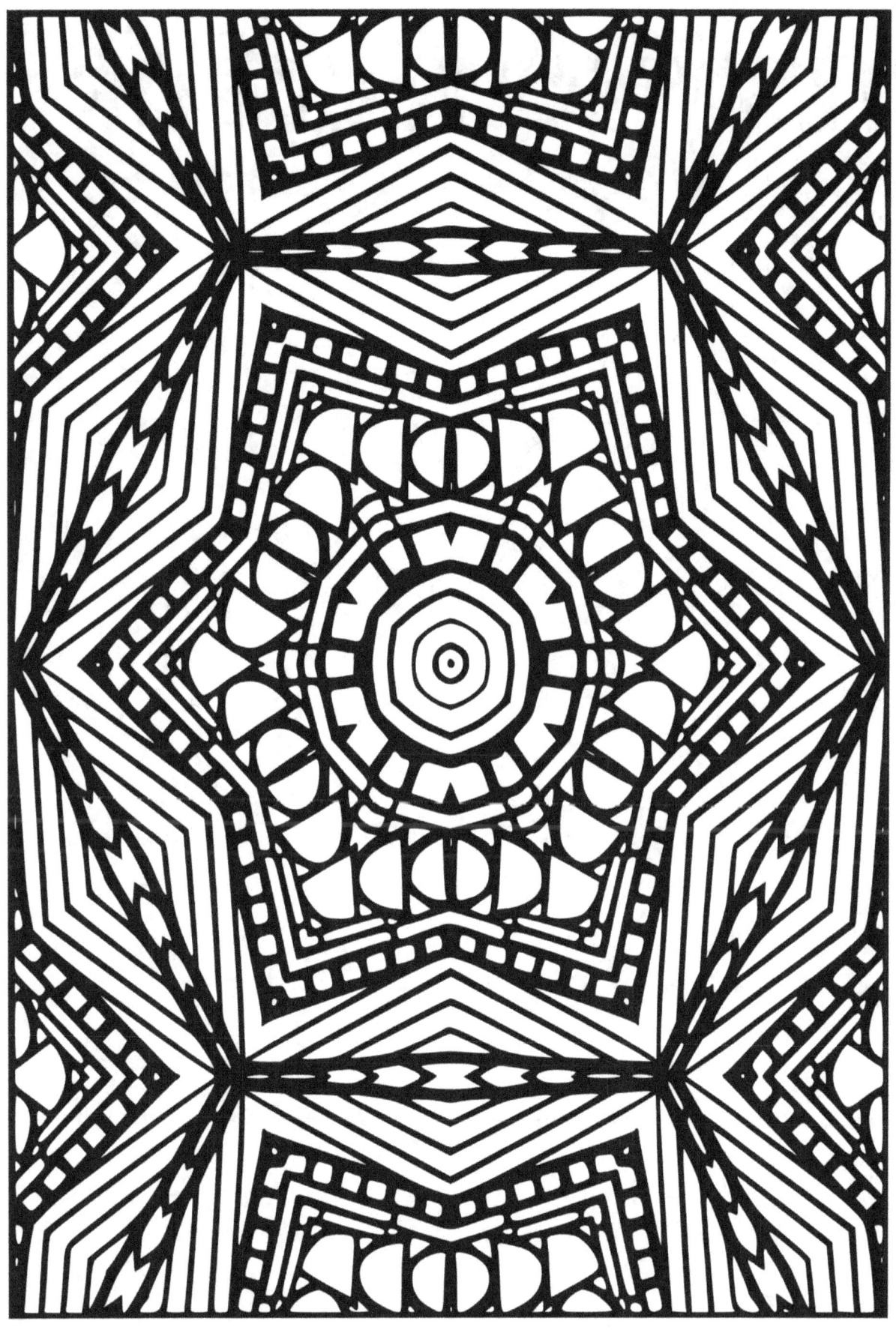

TEST YOUR COLOR

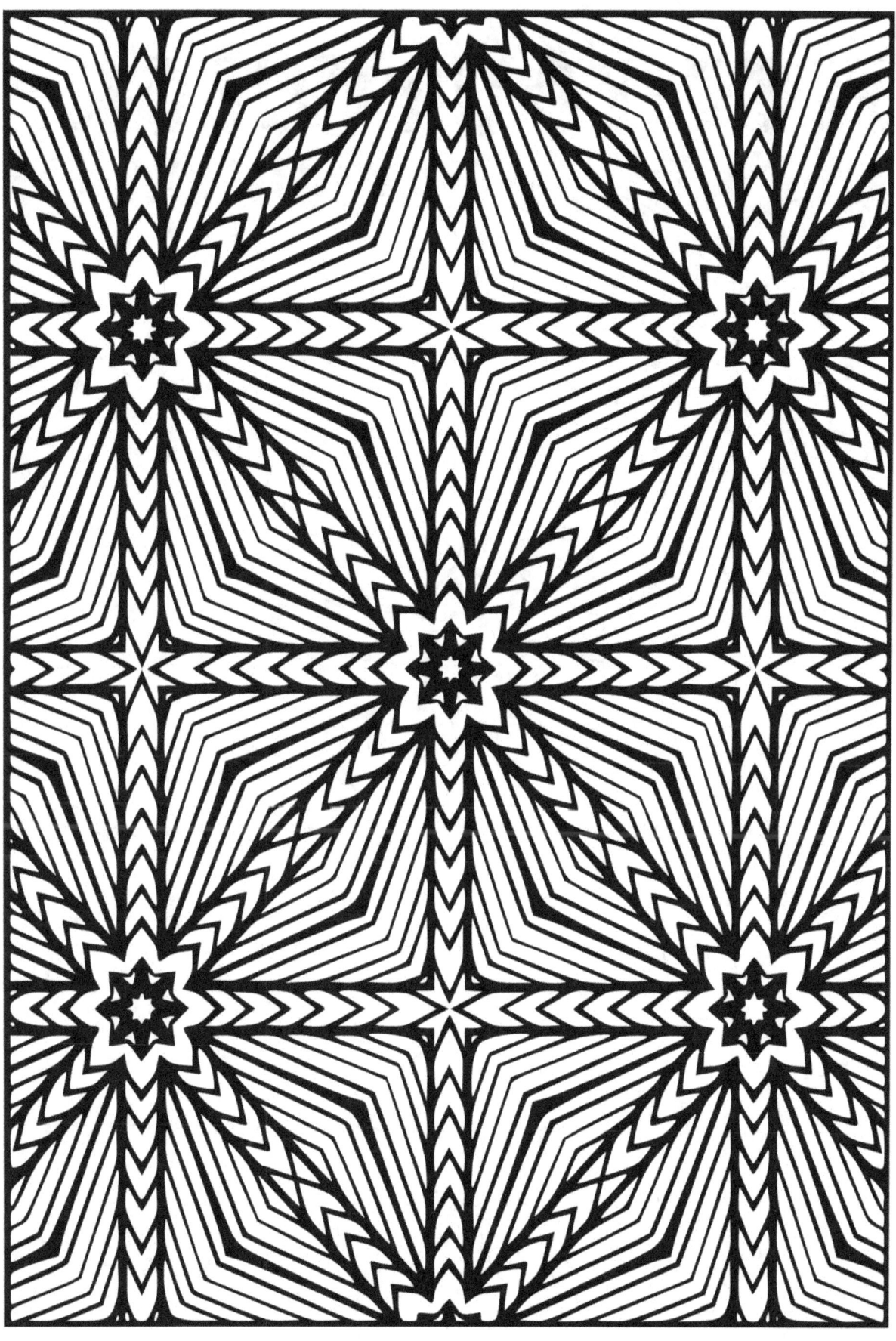

TEST YOUR COLOR

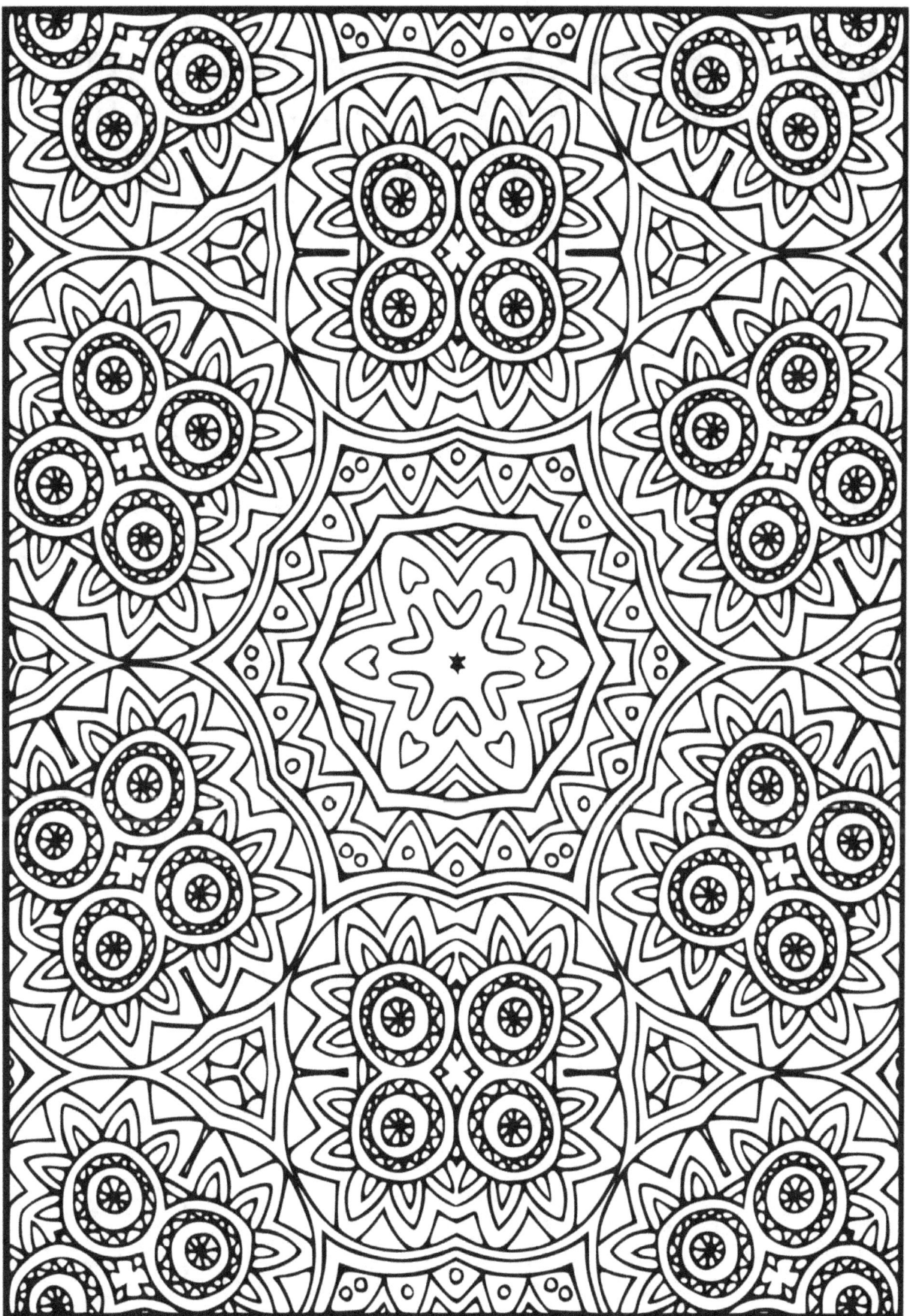

TEST YOUR COLOR

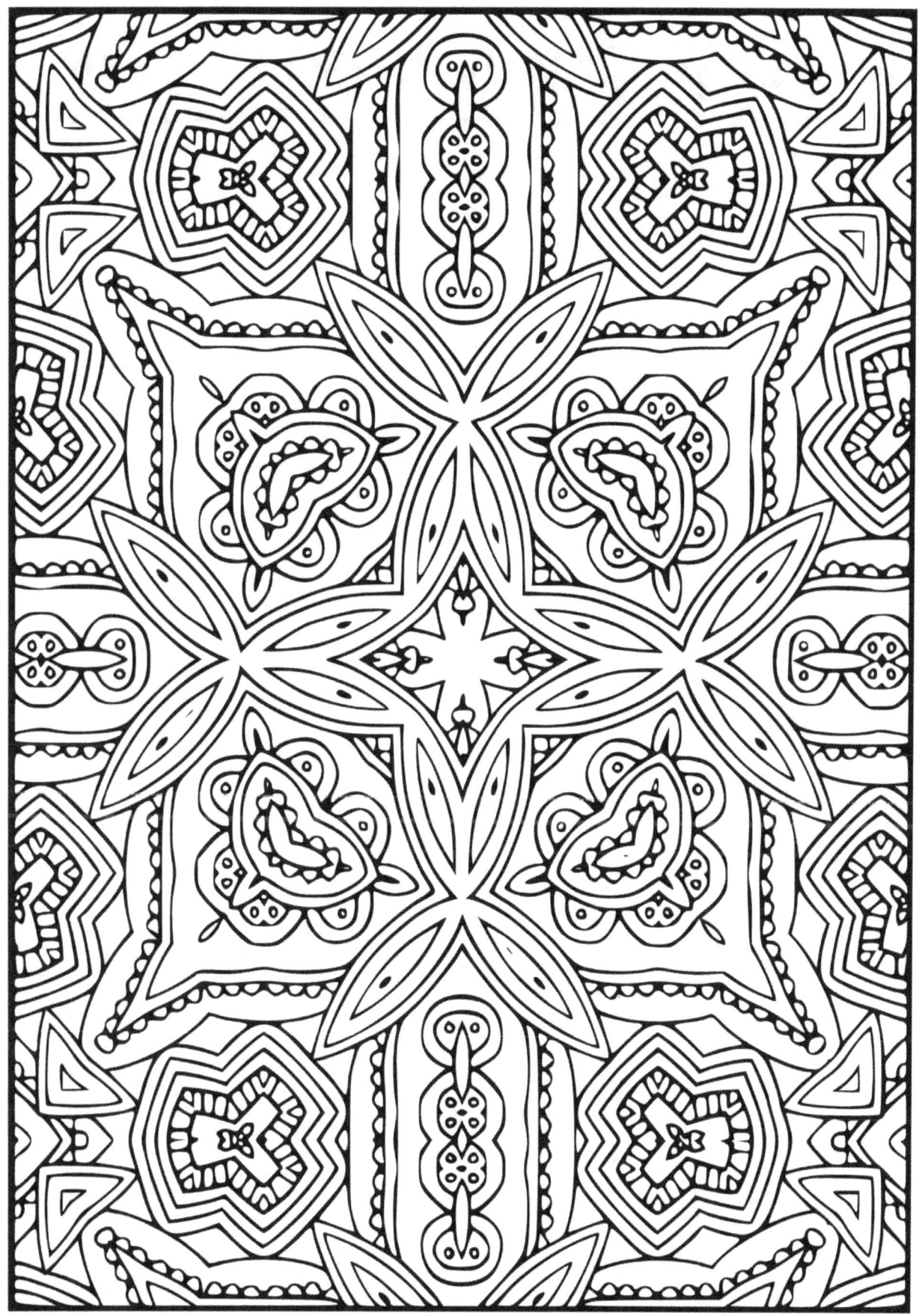

TEST YOUR COLOR

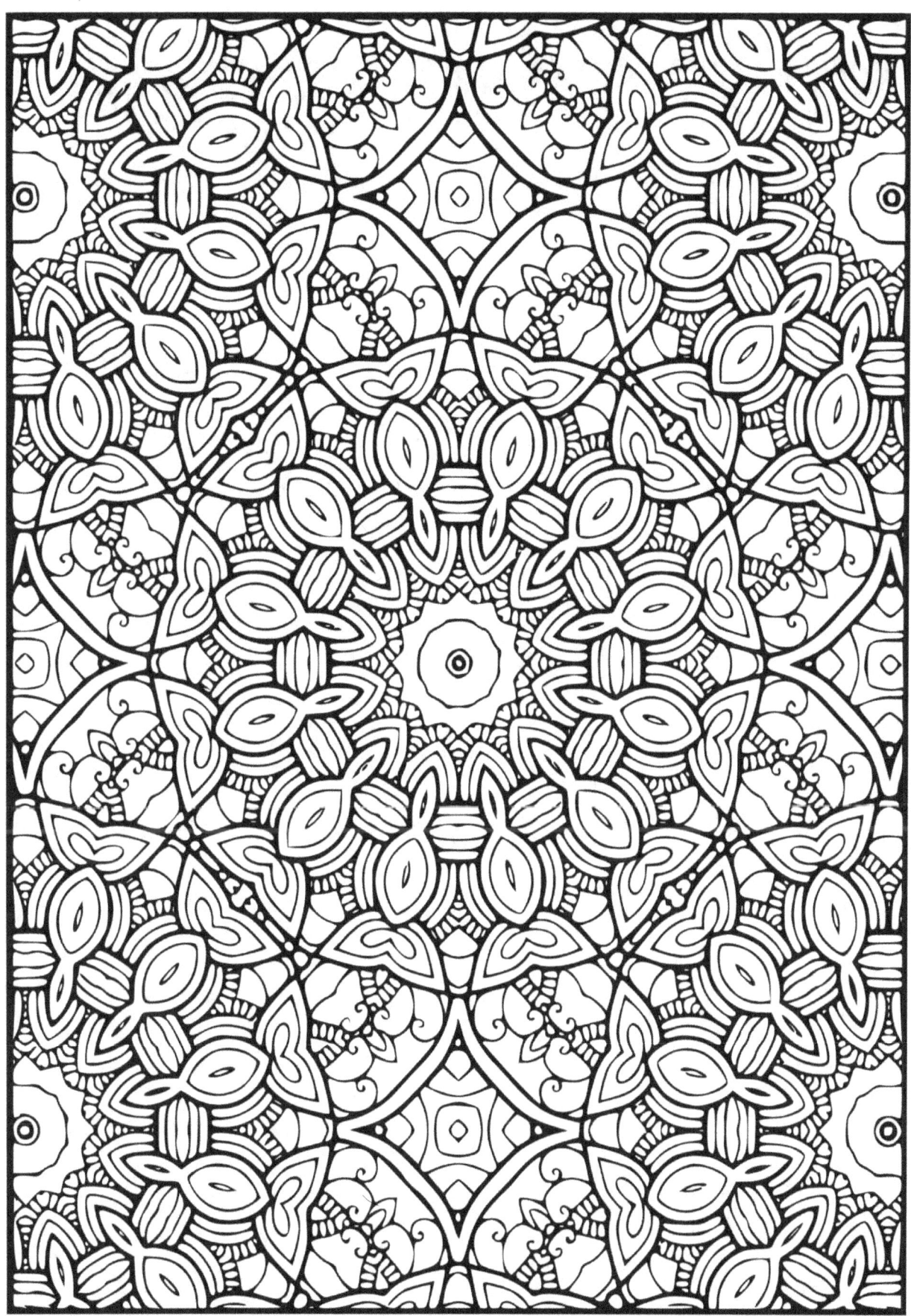

TEST YOUR COLOR

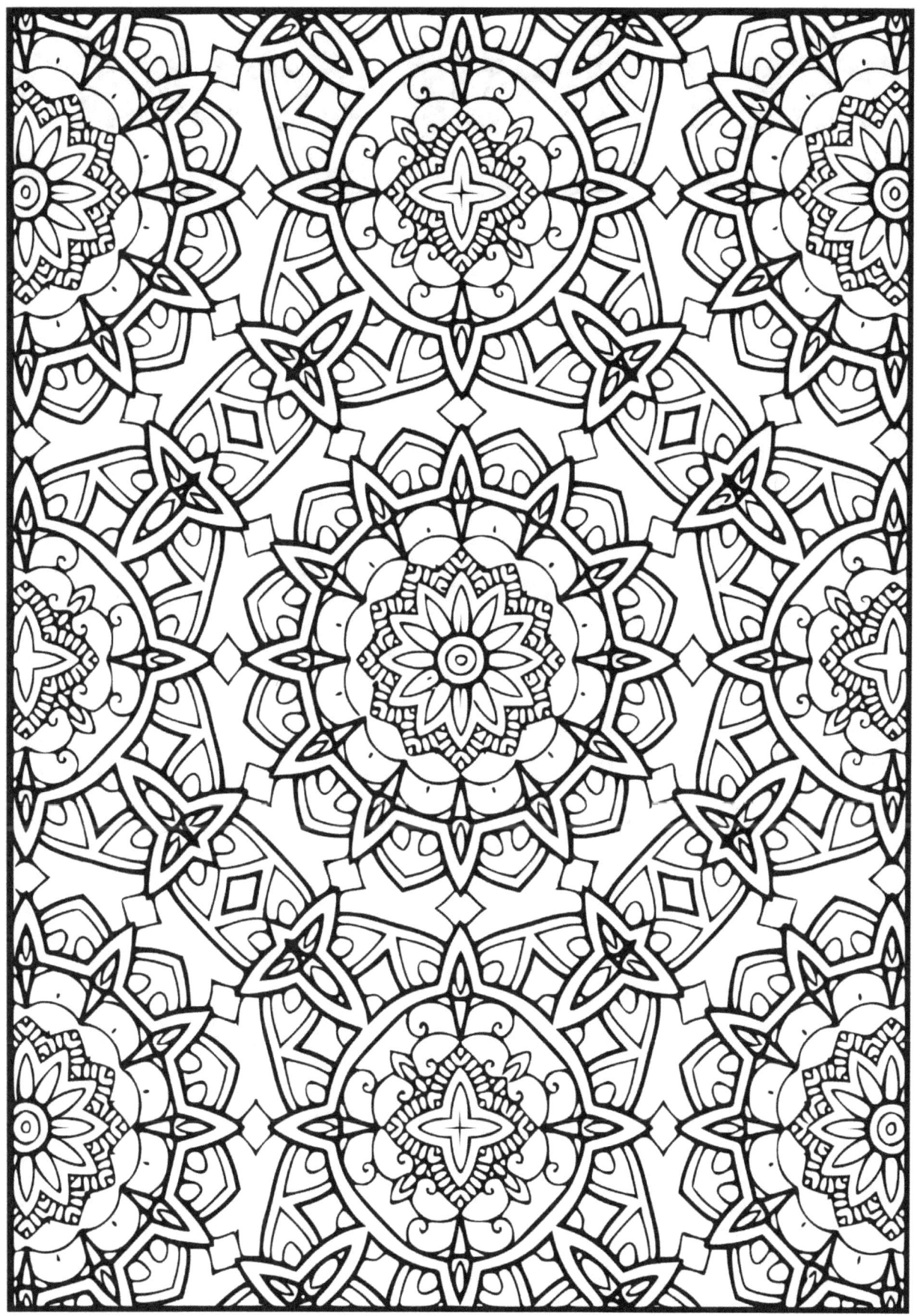

TEST YOUR COLOR

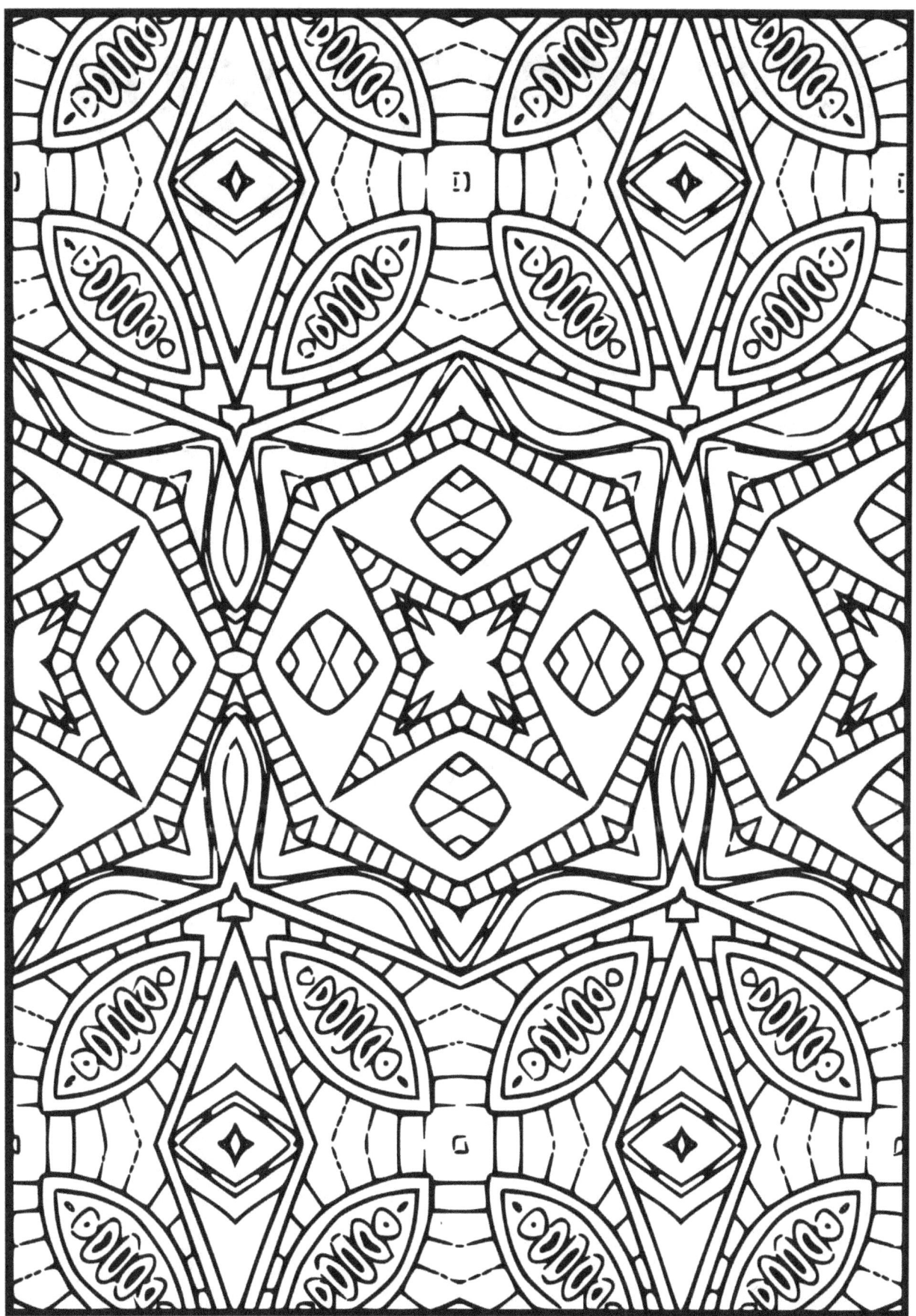

TEST YOUR COLOR

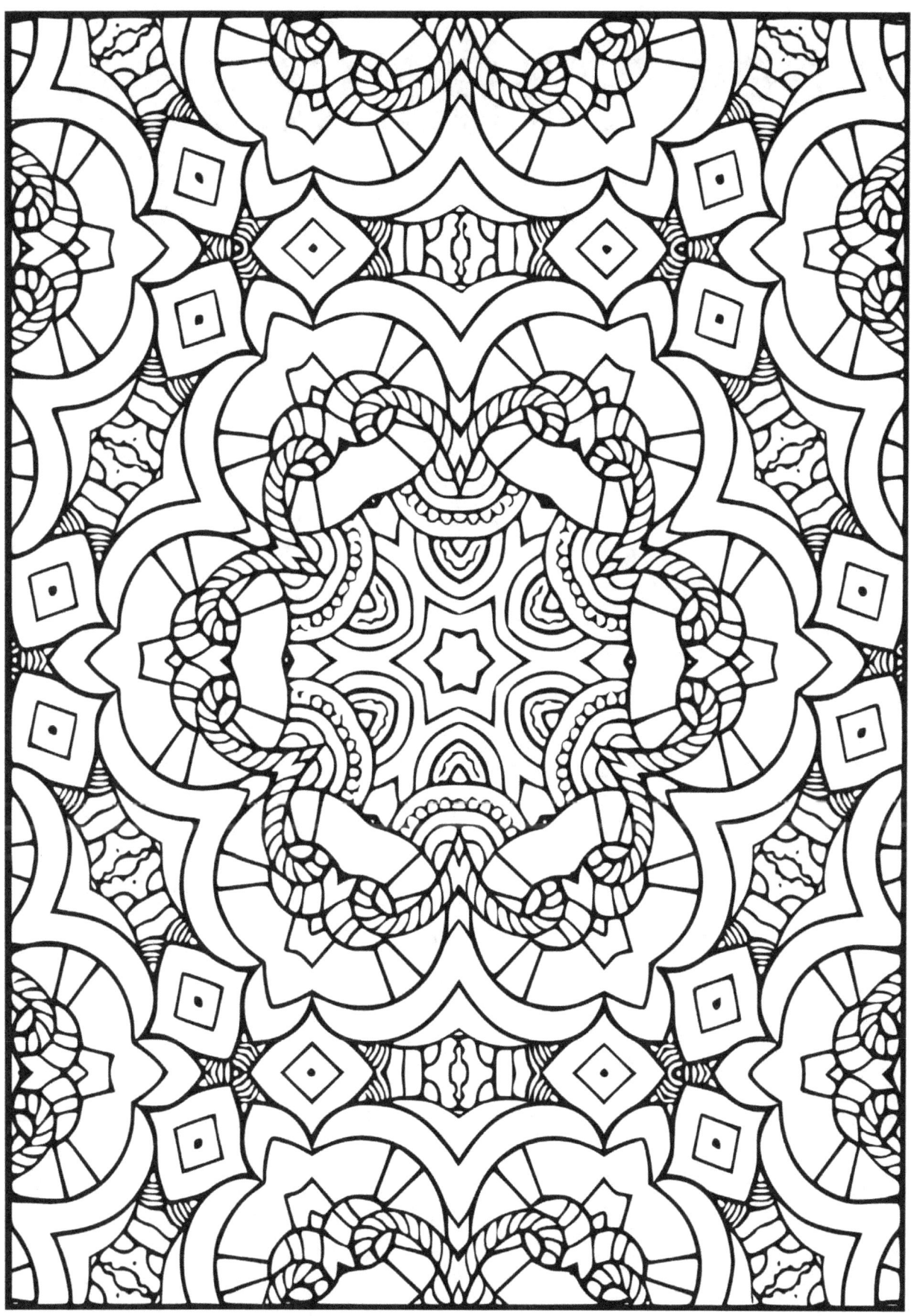

TEST YOUR COLOR

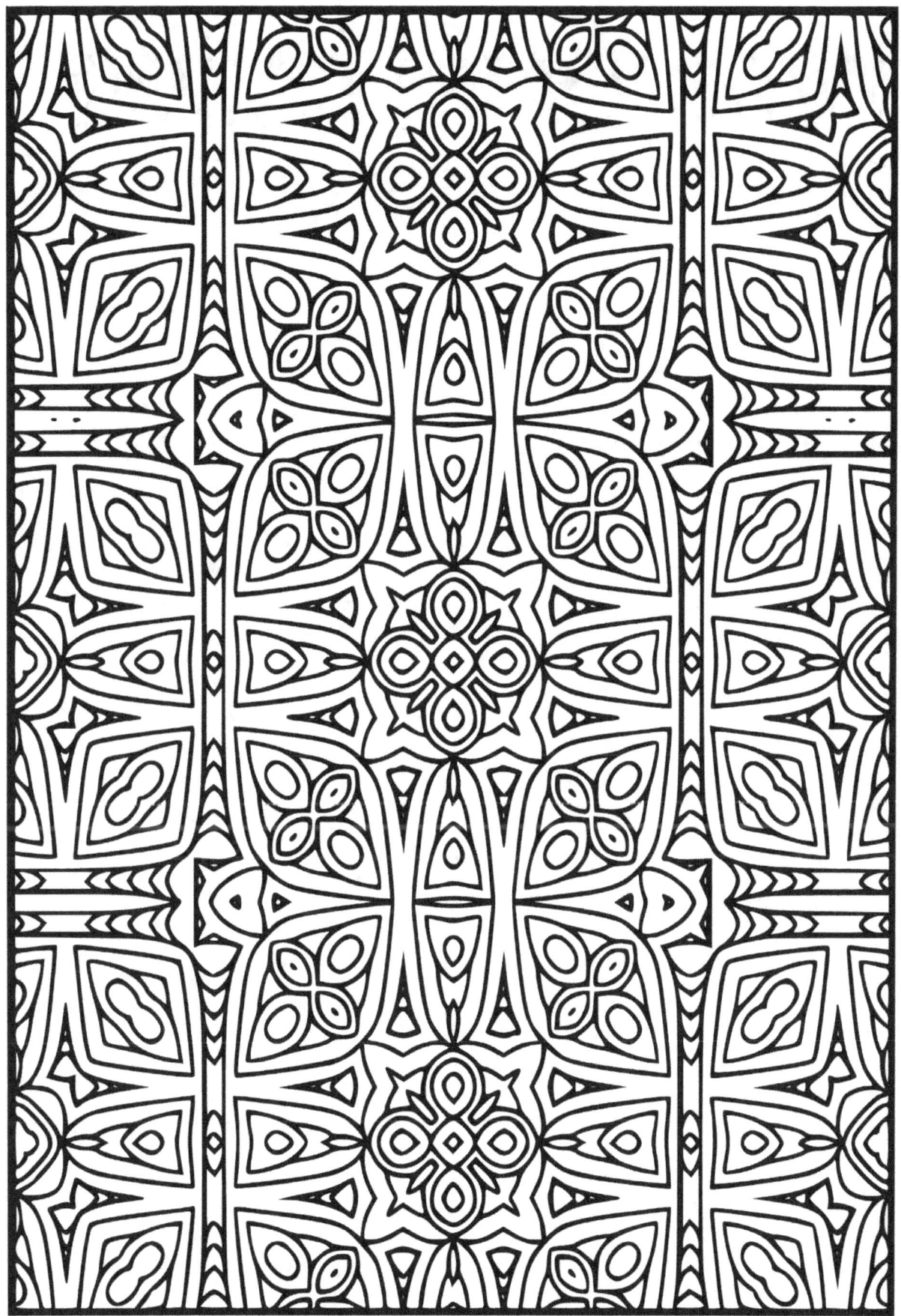

TEST YOUR COLOR

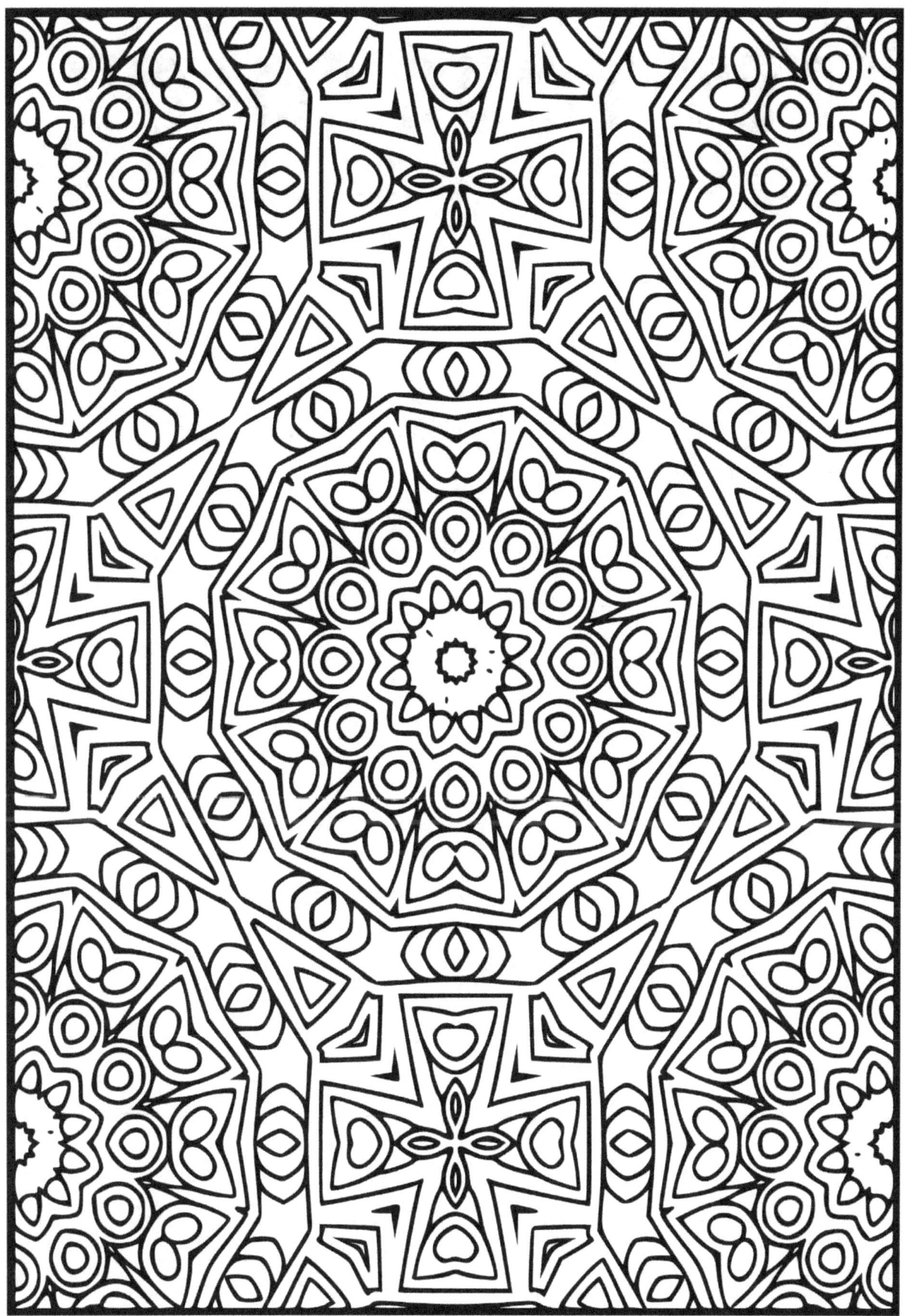

TEST YOUR COLOR

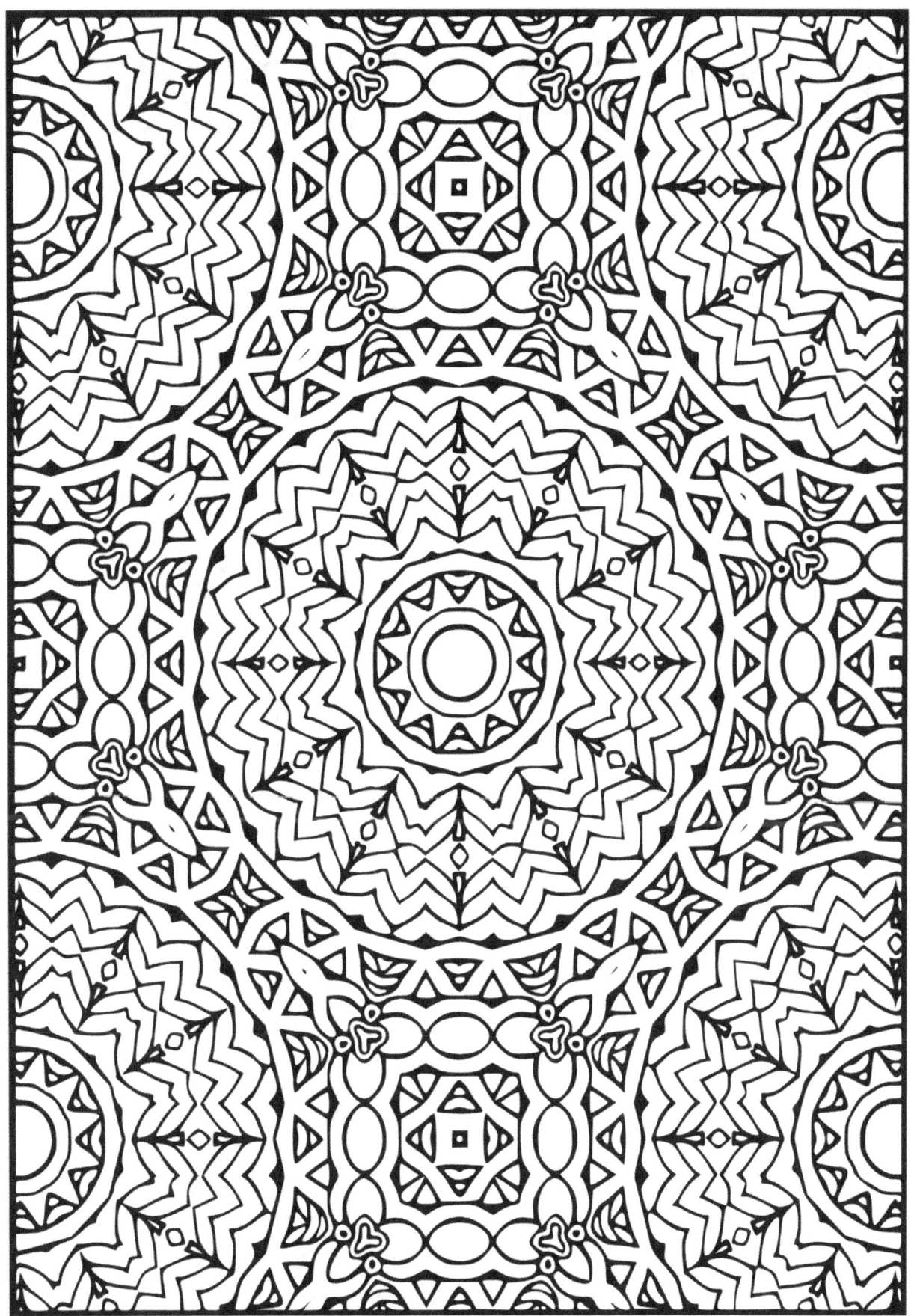

TEST YOUR COLOR

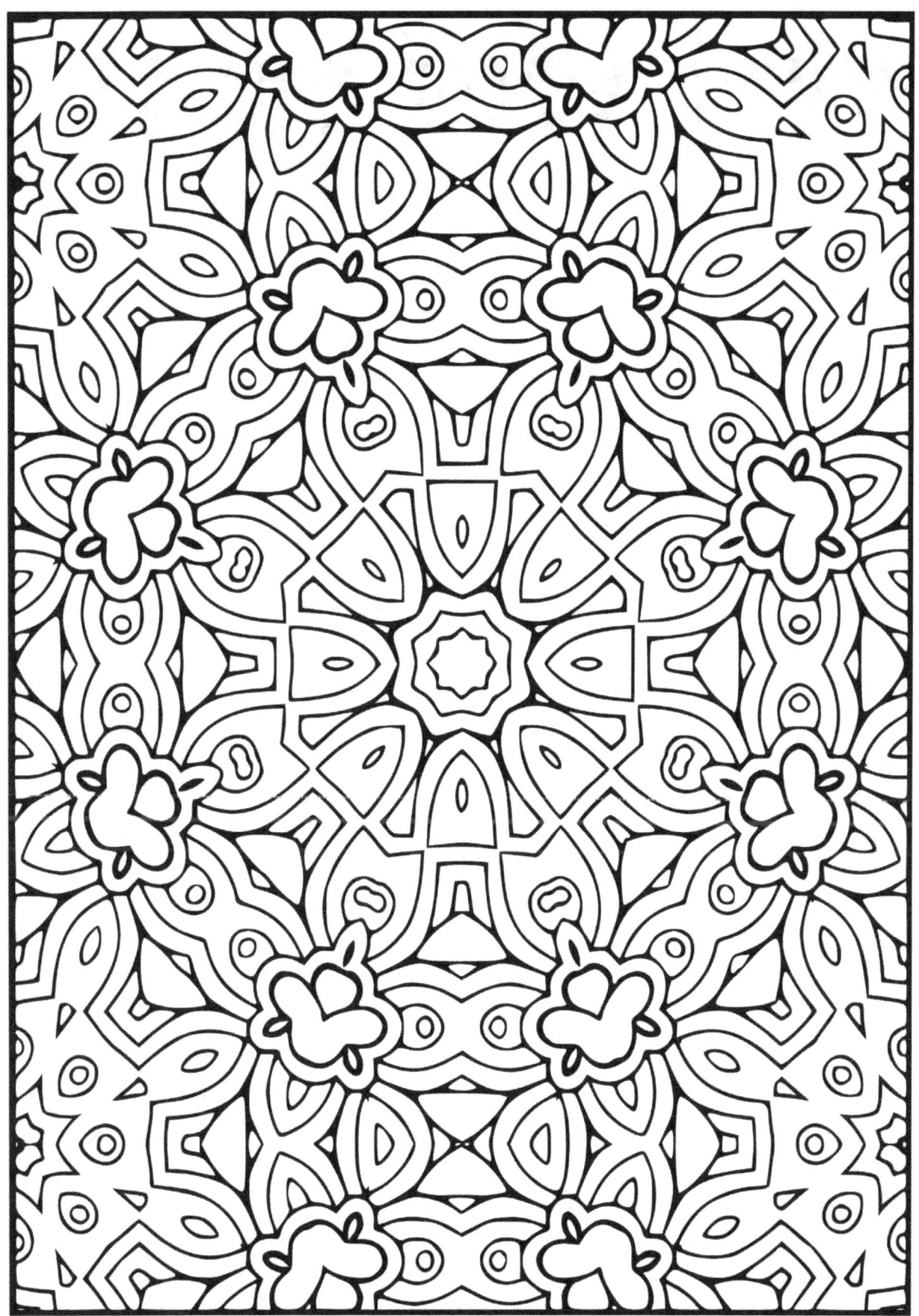

TEST YOUR COLOR

www.ingramcontent.com/pod-product-compliance
Lightning Source LLC
Chambersburg PA
CBHW082151230526
45467CB00044B/2847